"Deer!" he whispered, pointing. "Get off an' smoke 'em up!"

Something shot through me—a different kind of thrill. Ahead in the open I saw gray, graceful, wild forms trotting away. Like a flash I slid off my horse and jerked out the rifle. I ran forward a·few steps. The deer had halted—were gazing at us with heads up and ears high. What a wild and beautiful picture! As I raised my rifle they seemed to move and vanish in the green. The hunter in me, roused at last, anathematized my miserable luck. I ran ahead another few steps, to be halted by Copple. "Buck!" he called, sharply. "Hurry!" Then, out in the open sunlight, I saw a noble stag, moving, trotting toward us . . .

ZANE GREY · Volume 2
TALES OF LONELY TRAILS

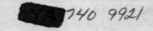

CHARTER BOOKS, NEW YORK

FRONTISPIECE. Zane Grey

All photographs are from the family collection of Zane Grey
and are the property of Zane Grey Incorporated.

This Charter book contains the complete
text of the second half of the original edition.
It has been completely reset in a typeface
designed for easy reading and was printed
from new film.

TALES OF LONELY TRAILS
VOLUME 2

A Charter Book/published by arrangement with
Northland Press

PRINTING HISTORY
Harper and Brothers edition published 1922
Northland Press edition published 1986
Charter edition/June 1988

ISBN: 1-55773-027-X

Charter Books are published by The Berkley Publishing Group,
200 Madison Avenue, New York, New York 10016.
The name "CHARTER" and the "C" logo
are trademarks belonging to Charter Communications, Inc.
PRINTED IN THE UNITED STATES OF AMERICA

10 9 8 7 6 5 4 3 2 1

Contents

CHAPTER ONE

Tonto Basin

The start of a camping trip, the getting a big outfit together and packed, and on the move, is always a difficult and laborsome job. Nevertheless, for me the preparation and the actual getting under way have always been matters of thrilling interest. This start of my hunt in Arizona, September 24, 1918, was particularly momentous because I had brought my boy Romer with me for his first trip into the wilds.

It may be that the boy was too young for such an undertaking. His mother feared he would be injured; his teachers presaged his utter ruin; his old nurse, with whom he waged war until he was free of her, averred that the best it could do for him would be to show what kind of stuff he was made of. His uncle R. C. was stoutly in favor of taking him. I believe the balance fell in Romer's favor when I remembered my own boyhood. As a youngster of three I had babbled of "bars an' buffers," and woven fantastic and marvelous tales of fiction about my imagined adventures—a habit, alas! I have never yet outgrown.

Anyway we only made six miles' travel on this September twenty-fourth, and Romer was with us.

Indeed he was omnipresent. His keen, eager joy communicated itself to me. Once he rode up alongside me and said: "Dad, this's great, but I'd rather do like Buck Duane." The boy had read all of my books, in spite of parents and

1

teachers, and he knew them by heart, and invariably liked the outlaws and gunmen best of all.

We made camp at sunset, with a flare of gold along the west, and the Peaks rising rosy and clear to the north. We camped in a cut-over pine forest, where stumps and lopped tops and burned deadfalls made an aspect of blackened desolation. From a distance, however, the scene was superb. At sunset there was a faint wind which soon died away.

My old guide on so many trips across the Painted Desert was in charge of the outfit. He was a wiry, gray, old pioneer, over seventy years, hollow-cheeked and bronzed, with blue-gray eyes still keen with fire. He was no longer robust, but he was tireless and willing. When he told a story he always began: "In the early days—" His son Lee had charge of the horses of which we had fourteen, two teams and ten saddle horses. Lee was a typical westerner of many occupations—cowboy, rider, rancher, cattleman. He was small, thin, supple, quick, tough and strong. He had a bronzed face, always chapped, a hooked nose, gray-blue eyes like his father's, sharp and keen.

Lee had engaged the only man he could find for a cook—Joe Isbel, a tall, lithe cowboy, straight as an Indian, with powerful shoulders, round limbs, and slender waist, and Isbel was what the westerners called a broncho-buster. He was a prize-winning rider at all the rodeos. Indeed, his seat in the saddle was individual and incomparable. He had a rough red-blue face, hard and rugged, like the rocks he rode over so fearlessly, and his eyes were bright hazel, steady and hard. Isbel's vernacular was significant. Speaking of one of our horses he said: "Like a mule he'll be your friend for twenty years to git a chance to kick you." Speaking of another that had to be shod he said: "Shore, he'll step high to-morrow." Isbel appeared to be remarkably efficient as camp-rustler and cook, but he did not inspire me with confidence. In speaking of this to the Doyles I found them non-committal on the subject. Westerners have sensitive feelings. I could not tell whether they were offended or not, and I half regretted mentioning my lack of confidence in Isbel. As it turned out, however, I was amply justified.

Sievert Nielsen, whom I have mentioned elsewhere, was the fourth of my men.

Darkness had enveloped us at supper time. I was tired out, but the red-embered camp-fire, the cool air, the smell of wood-smoke, and the white stars kept me awake awhile. Romer had to be put to bed. He was wild with excitement. We had had a sleeping-bag made for him so that once snugly in it, with the flaps buckled he could not kick off the blankets. When we got him into it he quieted down and took exceeding interest in his first bed in the open. He did not, however, go quickly to sleep. Presently he called R. C. over and whispered: "Say, Uncle Rome, I coiled a lasso an' put it under Nielsen's bed. When he's asleep you go pull it. He's tenderfoot like Dad was. He'll think it's a rattlesnake." This trick Romer must have remembered from reading "The Last of the Plainsmen," where I related what Buffalo Jones' cowboys did to me. Once Romer got that secret off his mind he fell asleep.

The hour we spent sitting around the camp-fire was the most pleasant of that night, though I did not know it then. The smell of wood-smoke and the glow of live coals stirred memories of other camp-fires. I was once more enveloped by the sweetness and peace of the open, listening to the sigh of the wind, and the faint tinkle of bells on the hobbled horses.

An uncomfortable night indeed it turned out to be. Our covers were scanty and did not number among them any blankets. The bed was hard as a rock, and lumpy. No sleep! As the night wore on the air grew colder, and I could not keep warm. At four A.M. I heard the howling of coyotes—a thrilling and well remembered wild chorus. After that perfect stillness reigned. Presently I saw the morning star—big, blue-white, beautiful. Uncomfortable hours seemed well spent if the reward was sight of the morning star. How few people ever see it! How very few ever get a glimpse of it on a desert dawn!

Just then, about five-thirty, Romer woke up and yelled lustily: "Dad! My nose's froze." This was a signal for me to laugh, and also to rise heroically. Not difficult because I wanted to stay in bed, but because I could hardly crawl out!

Soon we had a fire roaring. At six the dawn was still gray. Cold and nipping air, frost on everything, pale stars, a gold-red light in the east were proofs that I was again in the open. Soon a rose-colored flush beautified the Peaks.

After breakfast we had trouble with the horses. This always happened. But it was made worse this morning because a young cowboy who happened along took upon himself the task of helping Lee. I suspected he wanted to show off a little. In throwing his lasso to rope one, the noose went over the heads of two. Then he tried to hold both animals. They dragged him, pulled the lasso out of his hands, and stampeded the other horses. These two roped together thundered off with the noose widening. I was afraid they would split round a tree or stump, but fortunately the noose fell off one. As all the horses pounded off I heard Romer remark to Isbel: "Say, Joe, I don't see any medals on that cowboy." Isbel roared, and said: "Wal, Romer, you shore hit the nail on the haid!"

Owing to that stampede we did not get saddled and started till eleven o'clock. At first I was so sore and stiff from the hard bed that I rode a while on the wagon with Doyle. Many a mile I had ridden with him, and many a story he had related. This time he told about sitting on a jury at Prescott where they brought in as evidence bloody shirts, overalls, guns, knives, until there was such a pile that the table would not hold them. Doyle was a mine of memories of the early days.

Romer's mount was a little black, white-spotted horse named Rye. Lee Doyle had scoured the ranches to get this pony for the youngster. Rye was small for a horse, about the size of an Indian mustang, and he was gentle, as well as strong and fast. Romer had been given riding lessons all that summer in the east, and upon his arrival at Flagstaff he informed me that he could ride. I predicted he would be in the wagon before noon of the second day out. He offered to bet on it. I told him I disapproved of betting. He seemed to me to be daring, adaptable, self-willed; and I was divided between pride and anxiety as to the outcome of this trip for him.

In the afternoon we reached Lake Mary, a long, ugly,

muddy pond in a valley between pine-slopes. Dead and ghastly trees stood in the water, and the shores were cattle-tracked. Probably to the ranchers this mud-hole was a pleasing picture, but to me, who loved the beauty of the desert before its productiveness, it was hideous. When we passed Lake Mary, and farther on the last of the cut-over timber-land, we began to get into wonderful country. We traveled about sixteen miles, rather a small day's ride. Romer stayed on his horse all through that ride, and when we selected a camp site for the night he said to me: "Well, you're lucky you wouldn't bet."

Camp that evening was in a valley with stately pines straggling down to the level. On the other slope the pines came down in groups. The rim of this opposite slope was high, rugged, iron-colored, with cracks and holes. Before supper I walked up the slope back of our camp, to come upon level, rocky ground for a mile, then pines again leading to a low, green mountain with lighter patches of aspen. The level, open strip was gray in color. Arizona color and Arizona country! Gray of sage, rocks, pines, cedars, piñons, heights and depths and plains, wild and open and lonely—that was Arizona.

That night I obtained some rest and sleep, lying awake only a few hours, during which time I turned from side to side to find a soft place in the hard bed. Under such circumstances I always thought of the hard beds of the Greeks and the Spartans. Next day we rode twenty-three miles. On horseback trips like this it was every one for himself. Sometimes we would be spread out, all separated; at others we would be bunched; and again we would ride in couples. The morning was an ordeal for me, as at first I could scarcely sit my saddle; in the afternoon, however, riding grew to be less severe. The road led through a winding, shallow valley, with clumps of pine here and there, and cedars on the slopes. Romer rode all the way, half the time with his feet out of the stirrups, like a western boy born to the saddle, and he wanted to go fast all the time. Camp was made at a place called Fulton Spring. It might have been a spring once, but now it was a mud-hole with a dead cow lying in it. Clear, cold water is necessary to my pleasure, if not to my health. I have lived on sheep water—the water holes being tainted by sheep—and alkali water and soapy water of the desert, but never happily. How I hailed the clear, cold, swiftly-flowing springs!

This third camp lay in a woods where the pines were beautiful and the silence noticeable. Upon asking Romer to enumerate the things I had called to his attention, the few times I could catch up with him on the day's journey, he promptly replied—two big spiders—tarantulas, a hawk, and Mormon Lake. This lake was another snow-melted mud-hole, said to contain fish. I doubted that. Perhaps the little bull-head catfish might survive in such muddy water, but I did not believe bass or perch could.

One familiar feature of Arizona travel manifested itself to me that day—the dry air. My nails became brittle and my lips began to crack. I have had my lips cracked so severely that when I tried to bite bread they would split and bleed and hurt so that I could not eat. This matter of sore lips was for long a painful matter. I tried many remedies, and finally found one, camphor ice, that would prevent the drying and cracking.

Next day at dawn the forest was full of the soughing of wind in the pines—a wind that presaged storm. No stars showed. Romer-boy piled out at six o'clock. I had to follow him. The sky was dark and cloudy. Only a faint light showed in the east and it was just light enough to see when we ate breakfast. Owing to strayed horses we did not get started till after nine o'clock.

Five miles through the woods, gradually descending, led us into an open plain where there was a grass-bordered pond full of ducks. Here appeared an opportunity to get some meat. R. C. tried with shotgun and I with rifle, all to no avail. These ducks were shy. Romer seemed to evince some disdain at our failure, but he did not voice his feelings. We found some wild-turkey tracks, and a few feathers, which put our hopes high.

Crossing the open ground we again entered the forest, which gradually grew thicker as we got down to a lower altitude. Oak trees began to show in swales. And then we soon began to see squirrels, big, plump, gray fellows, with bushy tails almost silver. They appeared wilder than we would have suspected, at that distance from the settlements. Romer was eager to hunt them, and with his usual persistence, succeeded at length in persuading his uncle to do so.

To that end we rode out far ahead of the wagon and horses. Lee had a yellow dog he called Pups, a close-haired, keen-faced, muscular canine to which I had taken a dislike. To be fair to Pups, I had no reason except that he barked all the time. Pups and his barking were destined to make me hail them both with admiration and respect, but I had no idea of that then. Now this dog of Lee's would run ahead of us, trail squirrels, chase them, and tree them, whereupon he would bark vociferously. Sometimes up in the bushy top we would fail to spy the squirrel, but we had no doubt one was there. Romer wasted many and many a cartridge of the .22 Winchester trying to hit a squirrel. He had practiced a good deal, and was a fairly good shot for a youngster, but hitting a little gray ball of fur high on a tree, or waving at the tip of a branch, was no easy matter.

"Son," I said, "you don't take after your Dad."

And his uncle tried the lad's temper by teasing him about Wetzel. Now Wetzel, the great Indian killer of frontier days, was Romer's favorite hero.

"Gimme the .20 gauge," finally cried Romer, in desperation, with his eyes flashing.

Whereupon his uncle handed him the shotgun, with a word of caution as to the trigger. This particular squirrel was pretty high up, presenting no easy target. Romer stood almost directly under it, raised the gun nearly straight up, waved and wobbled and hesitated, and finally fired. Down sailed the squirrel to hit with a plump. That was Romer's first successful hunting experience. How proud he was of that gray squirrel! I suffered a pang to see the boy so radiant, so full of fire at the killing of a beautiful creature of the woods. Then again I remembered my own first sensations. Boys are blood-thirsty little savages. In their hunting, playing, even their reading, some element of the wild brute instinct dominates them. They are worthy descendants of progenitors who had to fight and kill to live. This incident furnished me much food for reflection. I foresaw that before this trip was ended I must face some knotty problems. I hated to shoot a squirrel even when I was hungry. Probably that was because I was not hungry enough. A starving man suffers no compunctions at the spilling of blood. On the contrary he revels in it with a fierce, primitive joy.

"Some shot, I'll say!" declared Romer to his uncle, loftily. And he said to me half a dozen times: "Say, Dad, wasn't it a grand peg?"

But toward the end of that afternoon his enthusiasm waned for shooting, for anything, especially riding. He kept asking when the wagon was going to stop. Once he yelled out: "Here's a peach of a place to camp." Then I asked him: "Romer, are you tired?" "Naw! But what's the use ridin' till dark?" At length he had to give up and be put on the wagon. The moment was tragic for him. Soon, however, he brightened at something Doyle told him, and began to ply the old pioneer with rapid-fire questions.

We pitched camp in an open flat, gray and red with short grass, and sheltered by towering pines on one side. Under these we set up our tents. The mat of pine needles was half a foot thick, soft and springy and fragrant. The woods appeared full of slanting rays of golden sunlight.

This day we had supper over before sunset. Romer showed no effects from his long, hard ride. First he wanted to cook, then he fooled around the fire, bothering Isbel. I had a hard time to manage him. He wanted to be eternally active. He teased and begged to go hunting—then he compromised on target practice. R. C. and I, however, were too tired, and we preferred to rest beside the camp-fire.

"Look here, kid," said R. C., "save something for to-morrow."

In disgust Romer replied: "Well, I suppose if a flock of antelope came along here you wouldn't move. . . . You an' Dad are great hunters, I don't think!"

After the lad had gone over to the other men R. C. turned to me and said reflectively: "Does he remind you of us when we were little?"

To which I replied with emotion: "In him I live over again!"

That is one of the beautiful things about children, so full of pathos and some strange, stinging joy—they bring back the days that are no more.

This evening, despite my fatigue, I was the last one to stay up. My seat was most comfortable, consisting of thick folds of blankets against a log. How the wind mourned in the trees! How the camp-fire sparkled, glowed red and white! Sometimes it seemed full of blazing opals. Always it held faces. And stories—more stories than I can ever tell! Once I was stirred and inspired by the beautiful effect of the pine trees in outline against the starry sky when the camp-fire blazed up. The color of the foliage seemed indescribably blue-green, something never seen by day. Every line shone bright, graceful, curved, rounded, and all thrown with sharp relief against the sky. How magical, exquisitely delicate and fanciful! The great trunks were soft serrated brown, and the gnarled branches stood out in perfect proportions. All works of art must be copies of nature.

Next morning early, while Romer slept, and the men had just begun to stir, I went apart from the camp out into the woods. All seemed solemn and still and cool, with the aisles of the forest brown and green and gold. I heard an owl, perhaps belated in his nocturnal habit. Then to my surprise I heard wild canaries. They were flying high, and to the south, going to their winter quarters. I wandered around among big, gray rocks and windfalls and clumps of young oak and majestic pines. More than one saucy red squirrel chattered at me.

When I returned to camp my comrades were at breakfast. Romer appeared vastly relieved to see that I had not taken a gun with me.

This morning we got an early start. We rode for hours through a beautiful shady forest, where a fragrant breeze in our faces made riding pleasant. Large oaks and patches of sumach appeared on the rocky slopes. We descended a good deal in this morning's travel, and the air grew appreciably warmer. The smell of pine was thick and fragrant; the sound of wind was sweet and soughing. Everywhere pine needles dropped, shining in the sunlight like thin slants of rain.

Only once or twice did I see Romer in all these morning hours; then he was out in front with the cowboy Isbel, riding his black pony over all the logs and washes he could find. I could see his feet sticking straight out almost even with his saddle. He did not appear to need stirrups. My fears gradually lessened.

During the afternoon the ride grew hot, and very dusty. We came to a long, open valley where the dust lay several inches deep. It had been an unusually dry summer and fall—a fact that presaged poor luck for our hunting—and the washes and stream-beds were bleached white. We came to two water-holes, tanks the Arizonians called them, and they were vile mud-holes with green scum on the water. The horses drank, but I would have had to be far gone from thirst before I would have slaked mine there. We faced west with the hot sun beating on us and the dust rising in clouds. No wonder that ride was interminably long.

At last we descended a canyon, and decided to camp in a level spot where several ravines met, in one of which a tiny stream of clear water oozed out of the gravel. The inclosure was rocky-sloped, full of caves and covered with pines; and the best I could say for it was that in case of storm the camp would be well protected. We shoveled out a deep hole in the gravel, so that it would fill up with water. Romer had evidently enjoyed himself this day. When I asked Isbel about him the cowboy's hard face gleamed with a smile: ''Shore thet kid's all right. He'll make a cowpuncher!'' His remark pleased me. In view of Romer's determination to emulate the worst bandit I ever wrote about I was tremendously glad to think of him as a cowboy. But as for myself I was tired, and the ride had been rather unprofitable, and this camp-site, to say the least, did not inspire me. It was neither wild nor beautiful nor comfortable. I went early to bed and slept like a log.

The following morning some of our horses were lost. The men hunted from daylight till ten o'clock. Then it was that I learned more about Lee's dog Pups. At ten-thirty Lee came in with the lost horses. They had hidden in a clump of cedars and remained perfectly quiet, as cute as deer. Lee put Pups on their trail. Pups was a horse-trailing dog and he soon found them. I had a change of feeling for Pups, then and there.

The sun was high and hot when we rode off. The pleasant and dusty stretches alternated. About one o'clock we halted on the edge of a deep wooded ravine to take our usual noonday rest. I scouted along the edge in the hope of seeing game of some kind. Presently I heard the cluck-cluck of turkeys. Slipping along to an open place I peered down to be thrilled by the sight of four good-sized turkeys. They were walking along the open strip of dry stream-bed at the bottom of the ravine. One was chasing grasshoppers. They were fairly close. I took aim at one, and thought I could have hit him, but suddenly I remembered Romer and R. C. So I slipped back and called them.

Hurriedly and stealthily we returned to the point where I had seen the turkeys. Romer had a pale face and wonderfully bright eyes; his actions resembled those of a stalking Indian. The turkeys were farther down, but still in plain sight. I told R. C. to take the boy and slip down, and run and hide and run till they got close enough for a shot. I would keep to the edge of the ravine.

Some moments later I saw R. C. and the boy running and stooping and creeping along the bottom of the ravine. Then I ran myself to reach a point opposite the turkeys, so in case they flew uphill I might get a shot. But I did not see them, and nothing happened. I lost sight of the turkeys. Hurrying back to where I had tied my horse I mounted him and loped ahead and came out upon the ravine some distance above. Here I hunted around for a little while. Once I heard the report of the .20 gauge, and then several rifle shots. Upon returning I found that Lee and Nielsen had wasted some shells. R. C. and Romer came wagging up the hill, both red and wet and tired. R. C. carried a small turkey, about the size of a chicken. He told me, between pants, that they chased the four large turkeys, and were just about to get a shot when up jumped a hen-turkey with a flock of young ones. They ran every way. He got one. Then he told me, between more pants and some laughs, that Romer had chased the little turkeys all over the ravine, almost catching several. Romer said for himself: "I just almost pulled feathers out of their tails. Gee! if I'd had a gun!"

We resumed our journey. About the middle of the afternoon Doyle called my attention to an opening in the forest through which I could see the yellow-walled rim of the mesa, and the great blue void below. Arizona! That explained the black forests, the red and yellow cliffs of rock, the gray cedars, the heights and depths.

Long ride indeed was it down off the mesa. The road was winding, rough full of loose rocks and dusty. We were all tired out trying to keep up with the wagon. Romer, however, averred time and again that he was not tired. Still I saw him often shift his seat from one side of the saddle to the other.

At last we descended to a comparative level and came to a little hamlet. Like all Mormon villages it had quaint log cabins, low stone houses, an irrigation ditch running at the side of the road, orchards, and many rosy-cheeked children. We lingered there long enough to rest a little and drink our fill of the cold granite water. I would travel out of my way to get a drink of water that came from granite rock.

About five o'clock we left for the Natural Bridge. Romer invited or rather taunted me to a race. When it ended in his victory I found that I had jolted my rifle out of its saddle sheath. I went back some distance to look for it, but did so in vain. Isbel said he would ride back in the morning and find it.

The country here appeared to be on a vast scale. But that was only because we had gotten out where we could see all around. Arizona is all on a grand, vast scale. Mountain ranges stood up to the south and east. North loomed up the lofty, steep rim of the Mogollon Mesa, with its cliffs of yellow and red, and its black line of timber. Westward lay fold on fold of low cedar-covered hills. The valley appeared a kind of magnificent bowl, rough and wild, with the distance lost in blue haze. The vegetation was dense and rather low. I saw both prickly-pear and mescal cactus, cedars, manzanita brush, scrub oak, and juniper trees. These last named were very beautiful, especially the smaller ones, with their gray-green foliage, and purple berries, and black and white checkered bark. There were no pine trees. Since we had left the rim above the character of plant life had changed.

We crossed the plateau leading to the valley where the

Natural Bridge was located. A winding road descended the east side of this valley. A rancher lived down there. Green of alfalfa and orchard and walnut trees contrasted vividly with a bare, gray slope on one side, and a red, rugged mountain on the other. A deep gorge showed dark and wild. At length, just after sunset, we reached the ranch, and rode through orchards of peach and pear and apple trees, all colored with fruit, and down through grassy meadows to a walnut grove where we pitched camp. By the time we had supper it was dark. Wonderful stars, thick, dreamy hum of insects, murmur of swift water, a rosy and golden afterglow on the notch of the mountain range to the west—these were inducements to stay up, but I was so tired I had to go to bed, where my eyelids fell tight, as if pleasantly weighted.

After the long, hard rides and the barren camp-sites what delight to awaken in this beautiful valley with the morning cool and breezy and bright, with smell of new-mown hay from the green and purple alfalfa fields, and the sunlight gilding the jagged crags above! Romer made a bee-line for the peach trees. He beat his daddy only a few yards. The kind rancher had visited us the night before and he had told us to help ourselves to fruit, melons, alfalfa. Needless to state that I made my breakfast on peaches!

I trailed the swift, murmuring stream to its source on the dark green slope where there opened up a big hole bordered by water-cress, long grass, and fragrant mint. This spring was one of perfectly clear water, six feet deep, boiling up to bulge on the surface. A grass of dark color and bunches of light green plant grew under the surface. Bees and blue dragon-flies hummed around and frogs as green as the grass blinked with jewelled eyes from the wet margins. The spring had a large volume that spilled over its borders with low, hollow gurgle, with fresh, cool splash. The water was soft, tasting of limestone. Here was the secret of the verdure and fragrance and color and beauty and life of the oasis.

It was also the secret of the formation of the wonderful Natural Bridge. Part of the rancher's cultivated land, to the extent of several acres, was the level top of this strange bridge. A meadow of alfalfa and a fine vineyard, in the air, like the hanging gardens of Babylon! The natural bridge spanned a deep gorge, at the bottom of which flowed a swift stream of water. Geologically this tremendous arch of limestone cannot be so very old. In comparatively recent times an earthquake or some seismic disturbance or some other natural force caused a spring of water to burst from the slope above the gorge. It ran down, of course, over the rim. The lime salt in the water was deposited, and year by year and age by age advanced toward the opposite side until a bridge crossed the gorge. The swift stream at the bottom kept the opening clear under the bridge.

A winding trail led deep down on the lower side of this wonderful natural span. It showed the cliffs of limestone, porous, craggy, broken, chalky. At the bottom the gorge was full of tremendous boulders, water-worn ledges, sycamore and juniper trees, red and yellow flowers, and dark, beautiful green pools. I espied tiny gray frogs, reminding me of those I found in the gulches of the Grand Canyon. Many huge black beetles, some alive, but most of them dead, lined the wet borders of the pools. A species of fish that resembled mullet lay in the shadow of the rocks.

From underneath the Natural Bridge showed to advantage, and if not magnificent like the grand Nonnezoshe of Utah, it was at least striking and beautiful. It had a rounded ceiling colored gray, yellow, green, bronze, purple, white, making a crude and scalloped mosaic. Water dripped from it like a rain of heavy scattered drops. The left side was dryest and large, dark caves opened up, one above the other, the upper being so high that it was dangerous to attempt reaching it. The right side was slippery and wet. All rocks were thickly encrusted with lime salt. Doyle told us that any object left under the ceaseless drip, drip of the lime water would soon become encrusted, and heavy as stone. The upper opening of the arch was much higher and smaller than the lower. Any noise gave forth strange and sepulchral echoes. Romer certainly made the welkin ring. A streak of sunlight shone through a small hole in the thinnest part of the roof. Doyle pointed out the high cave where Indians had once lived, showing the markings of their fire. Also he told a story of Apaches being driven into the highest cave from which they had never escaped. This tale was manifestly to Romer's liking and I had to use force to keep him from risking his neck. A very strong breeze blew under the arch. When we rolled a boulder into the large, dark pool it gave forth a hollow boom, boom, boom, growing hollower the deeper it went. I tried to interest Romer in some bat nests in crevices high up, but the boy wanted to roll stones and fish for the mullet. When we climbed out and were once more on a level I asked him what he thought of the place. "Some hole—I'll say!" he panted, breathlessly.

The rancher told me that the summer rains began there about July, and the snows about the first of the year. Snow never lay long on the lower slopes. Apaches had lived there forty years ago and had cultivated the soil. There was gold in the mountains of the Four Peaks Range. In this sheltered nook the weather was never severely cold or hot; and I judged from the quaint talk of the rancher's wife that life there was always afternoon.

Next day we rode from Natural Bridge to Payson in four and a half hours. Payson appeared to be an old hamlet, retaining many frontier characteristics such as old board and stone houses with high fronts, hitching posts and pumps on sidewalks, and one street so wide that it resembled a Mexican plaza. Payson contained two stores, where I hoped to buy a rifle, and hoped in vain. I had not recovered my lost gun, and when night came my prospects of anything to hunt with appeared extremely slim. But we had visitors, and one of them was a stalwart, dark-skinned rider named Copple, who introduced himself by saying he would have come a good way to meet the writer of certain books he had profited by. When he learned of the loss of my rifle and that I could not purchase one anywhere he pressed upon me his own. I refused with thanks, but he would not take no. The upshot of it was that he lent me his .30 Government Winchester, and gave me several boxes of ammunition. Also he presented me with a cowhide lasso. Whereupon Romer-boy took a shine to Copple at once. "Say, you look like an Indian," he declared. With a laugh Copple replied: "I am part Indian, sonny."

Manifestly that settled his status with Romer, for he piped up:
"So's Dad part Indian. You'd better come huntin' with us."

We had for next day to look forward to the longest and
hardest ride of the journey in, and in order to make it and
reach a good camping site I got up at three o'clock in the
morning to rout everybody out. It was pitch dark until we
kindled fires. Then everybody rustled to such purpose that we
were ready to start before dawn, and had to wait a little for
light enough to see where we were going. This procedure
tickled Romer immensely. I believed he imagined he was in a
pioneer caravan. The gray breaking of dawn, the coming of
brighter light, the rose and silver of the rising sun, and the
riding in its face, with the air so tangy and nipping, were
circumstances that inspired me as the adventurous start pleased
Romer. The brush and cactus-lined road was rough, up hill
and down, with ever increasing indications that it was seldom
used. From the tops of high points I could see black foothills,
round, cone-shaped, flat-topped, all leading the gaze toward
the great yellow and red wall of the mesa, with its fringed
borderline, wild and beckoning.

We walked our horses, trotted, loped, and repeated the
order, over and over, hour by hour, mile after mile, under a
sun that burned our faces and through choking dust. The
washes and stream-beds were bleached and dry; the brush was
sear and yellow and dust laden: the mescal stalks seemed
withered by hot blasts. Only the manzanita looked fresh. That
smooth red-branched and glistening green-leafed plant of the
desert apparently flourished without rain. On all sides the
evidences of extreme drought proved the year to be the
dreaded *anno seco* of the Mexicans.

For ten hours we rode without a halt before there was any
prominent change in the weary up- and downhill going, in the
heat and dust and brush-walled road. But about the middle of
the afternoon we reached the summit of the longest hill, from
which we saw ahead of us a cut up country, wild and rugged
and beautiful, with pine-sloped canyon at our feet. We heard
the faint murmur of running water. Hot, dusty, wet with
sweat, and thirsty as sheep, we piled down that steep slope as
fast as we dared. Our horses did not need urging. At the

bottom we plunged into a swift stream of clear, cold water—granite water—to drink of which, and to bathe hot heads and burning feet, was a joy only known to the weary traveler of the desert. Romer yelled that the water was like that at our home in the mountains of Pennsylvania, and he drank till I thought he would burst, and then I had to hold him to keep him from wallowing in it.

Here we entered a pine forest. Heat and dust stayed with us, and the aches and pains likewise, but the worst of them lay behind. Every mile grew shadier, clearer, cooler.

Nielsen happened to fall in and ride beside me for several miles, as was often his wont. The drink of water stirred him to an Homeric recital of one of his desert trips in Sonora, at the end of which, almost dead of thirst, he had suddenly come upon such a stream as the one we had just passed. Then he told me about his trips down the west coast of Sonora, along the Gulf, where he traveled at night, at low tide, so that by daytime his footprints would be washed out. This was the land of the Seri Indians. Undoubtedly these Indians were cannibals. I had read considerable about them, much of which ridiculed the rumors of their cannibalistic traits. This of course had been of exceeding interest to me, because some day I meant to go to the land of the Seris. But not until 1918 did I get really authentic data concerning them. Professor Bailey of the University of California told me he had years before made two trips to the Gulf, and found the Seris to be the lowest order of savages he knew of. He was positive that under favorable circumstances they would practice cannibalism. Nielsen made four trips down there. He claimed the Seris were an ugly tribe. In winter they lived on Tiburon Island, off which boats anchored on occasions, and crews and fishermen and adventurers went ashore to barter with the Indians. These travelers did not see the worst of the Seris. In summer they range up the mainland, and they go naked. They do not want gold discovered down there. They will fight prospectors. They use arrows and attack at dawn. Also they poison the water-holes.

Nielsen told of some men who were massacred by Seris on the mainland opposite Tiburon Island. One man, who had gone away from camp, returned to hear the attack upon his companions. He escaped and made his way to Gyamus. Procuring assistance this man returned to the scene of the massacre, only to find stakes in the sand, with deep trails tramped around them, and blackened remains of fires, and bones everywhere. Nielsen went on to say that once from a hiding place he had watched Seris tear up and devour a dead turtle that he afterward ascertained was putrid. He said these Seris were the greatest runners of all desert savages. The best of them could outrun a horse. One Seri, a giant seven feet tall, could outrun a deer and break its neck with his hands.

These statements of Nielsen's were remarkable, and personally I believed them. Men of his stamp were honest and they had opportunities to learn strange and terrible facts in nature. The great naturalist Darwin made rather stronger claims for the barbarism of the savages of Terra del Fuego. Nielsen, pursuing his theme, told me how he had seen, with his own eyes—and they were certainly sharp and intelligent—Yaqui Indians leap on the bare backs of wild horses and locking their legs, stick there in spite of the mad plunges and pitches. The Gauchos of the Patagonian Pampas were famous for that feat of horsemanship. I asked Joe Isbel what he thought of such riding. And he said: "Wal, I can ride a wild steer bare-back, but excoose me from tacklin' a buckin' bronch without saddle an' stirrups." This coming from the acknowledged champion horseman of the southwest was assuredly significant.

At five o'clock we came to the end of the road. It led to a forest glade, overlooking the stream we had followed, and that was as far as our wagon could go. The glade shone red with sumach, and surrounded by tall pines, with a rocky and shady glen below, it appeared a delightful place to camp. As I was about to unsaddle my horses I heard the cluck-cluck of turkeys. Pulling out my borrowed rifle, and calling Romer, I ran to the edge of the glade. The shady, swift stream ran fifty feet or so below me. Across it I saw into the woods where shade and gray rocks and colored brush mingled. Again I heard the turkeys cluck. "Look hard, son," I whispered. "They're close." R. C. came slipping along below us, with his rifle ready. Suddenly Romer stiffened, then pointed. "There! Dad!—There!" I saw two gobblers wade into the brook not more than a hundred and fifty feet away. Drawing down with fine aim I fired. The bullet splashed water all over the turkeys. One with loud whirr of wings flew away. The other leaped across the brook and ran—swift as a deer—right up the slope. As I tried to get the sight on him I heard other turkeys fly, and the crack-crack of R. C.'s gun. I shot twice at my running turkey, and all I did was to scatter the dirt over him, and make him run faster. R. C. had not done any better shooting. Romer, wonderful to relate, was so excited that he forgot to make fun of our marksmanship. We scouted around some, but the turkeys had gone. By promising to take Romer hunting after supper I contrived to get him back to the glade, where we made camp.

II

After we had unpacked and while the men were pitching the tents and getting supper I took Romer on a hunt up the creek. I was considerably pleased to see good-sized trout in the deeper pools. A little way above camp the creek forked. As the right-hand branch appeared to be larger and more attractive we followed its course. Soon the bustle of camp life and the sound of the horses were left far behind. Romer slipped along beside me stealthily as an Indian, all eyes and ears.

We had not traveled thus for a quarter of a mile when my quick ear caught the cluck-cluck of turkeys. "Listen," I whispered, halting. Romer became like a statue, his dark eyes dilating, his nostrils quivering, his whole body strung. He was a Zane all right. A turkey called again; then another answered. Romer started, and nodded his head vehemently.

"Come on now, right behind me," I whispered. "Step where I step and do what I do. Don't break any twigs."

Cautiously we glided up the creek, listening now and then to get the direction, until we came to an open place where we could see some distance up a ridge. The turkey clucks came from across the creek somewhere up this open aisle of the forest. I crawled ahead several rods to a more advantageous point, much pleased to note that Romer kept noiselessly at my heels. Then from behind a stone we peeped out. Almost at once a turkey flew down from a tree into the open lane. "Look Dad!" whispered Romer, wildly. I had to hold him down. "That's a hen turkey," I said. "See, it's small and dull-colored. The gobblers are big, shiny, and they have red on their heads."

Another hen turkey flew down from a rather low height. Then I made out grapevines, and I saw several animated dark patches among them. As I looked three turkeys flopped down to the ground. One was a gobbler of considerable size, with beautiful white and bronze feathers. Rather suspiciously he looked down our way. The distance was not more than a hundred yards. I aimed at him, feeling as I did so how Romer quivered beside me, but I had no confidence in Copple's rifle. The sights were wrong for me. The stock did not fit me. So, hoping for a closer and better shot, I let this opportunity pass. Of course I should have taken it. The gobbler clucked and began to trot up the ridge, with the others after him. They were not frightened, but they appeared rather suspicious. When they disappeared in the woods Romer and I got up, and hurried in pursuit. "Gee! why didn't you peg that gobbler?" broke out Romer, breathlessly. "Wasn't he a peach?"

When we reached the top of the ridge we advanced very cautiously again. Another open place led to a steep, rocky hillside with cedars and pines growing somewhat separated. I was disappointed in not seeing the turkeys. Then in our anxiety and eagerness we hurried on, not noiselessly by any means. All of a sudden there was a rustle, and then a great whirr of wings. Three turkeys flew like grouse away into the woods. Next I saw the white gobbler running up the rocky hillside. At first he was in the open. Aiming as best I could I waited for him to stop or hesitate. But he did neither. "Peg him, Dad!" yelled Romer. The lad was right. My best chance I had again forfeited. To hit a running wild turkey with a rifle bullet was a feat I had not done so often as to inspire conceit. The gobbler was wise, too. For that matter all grown gobblers are as wise as old bucks, except in the spring mating season, when it is a crime to hunt them. This one, just as I got a bead on him, always ran behind a rock or tree or shrub. Finally in desperation I took a snap shot at him, hitting under him, making him jump. Then in rapid succession I fired four more times. I had the satisfaction of seeing where my bullets struck up the dust, even though they did go wide of the mark. After my last shot the gobbler disappeared.

"Well, Dad, you sure throwed the dirt over him!" declared Romer.

"Son, I don't believe I could hit a flock of barns with this gun," I replied, gazing doubtfully at the old, shiny, wire-wrapped, worn-out Winchester Copple had lent me. I had been told that he was a fine marksman and could drive a nail with it. Upon my return to camp I tried out the rifle, carefully, with a rest, to find that it was not accurate. Moreover it did not throw the bullets consistently. It shot high, wide, low; and right there I abandoned any further use for it. R. C. tried to make me take his rifle to use on the hunting trip; Nielsen and Lee wanted me to take theirs, but I was disgusted with myself and refused. "Thanks, boys," I said. "Maybe this will be a lesson to me."

We had been up since three o'clock that morning, and the day's travel had been exhausting. I had just enough energy left to scrape up a huge, soft pile of pine needles upon which to make our bed. After that all was oblivion until I was awakened by the ringing strokes of Nielsen's axe.

The morning, after the sun got up, was exceedingly delightful. And this camp was such a contrast to the others, so pleasant and attractive, that even if we had not arranged to meet Lee Haught and his sons here I would have stayed a while anyway. Haught was a famed bear hunter who lived in a log-cabin somewhere up under the rim of the mesa. While Lee and Nielsen rode off up the trail to find Haught I gave Romer his first try at rainbow trout. The water of the creek was low and clear, so that we could see plenty of good-sized trout. But they were shy. They would not rise readily to any of our flies, though I got several strikes. We searched under the stones for worms and secured a few. Whereupon Romer threw a baited hook to a trout we plainly saw. The trout gobbled it. Romer had been instructed in the fine art of angling, but whenever he got a bite he always forgot science. He yanked this ten-inch rainbow right out. Then in another pool he hooked a big fellow that had ideas of his own as well as weight and strength. Romer applied the same strenuous tactics. But this trout nearly pulled Romer off the rock before the line broke. I took occasion then to deliver to the lad a lecture. In reply he said tearfully: "I didn't know he was so—so big."

When we retured to camp, Haught and his sons were there. Even at a distance their horses, weapons, and persons satisfied my critical eye. Lee Haught was a tall, spare, superbly built man, with square shoulders. He had a brown face with deep lines and sunken cheeks, keen hazel eyes, heavy dark mustache, and hair streaked a little with gray. The only striking features of his apparel were his black sombrero and long spurs.

His sons, Edd and George, were young, lean, sallow, still-faced, lanky-legged horsemen with clear gray eyes. They did not appear to be given to much speech. Both were then waiting for the call of the army draft. Looking at them then, feeling the tranquil reserve and latent force of these Arizonians, I reflected that the Germans had failed in their psychology of American character. A few hundred thousand Americans like the Haught boys would have whipped the German army.

We held a council. Haught said he would send his son Edd with Doyle, and by a long roundabout forest road get the wagon up on the mesa. With his burros and some of our horses packed we could take part of the outfit up the creek trail, past his cabin, and climb out on the rim, where we would find grass, water, wood, and plenty of game.

The idea of permanent camp before sunset that very day inspired us to united and vigorous effort. By noon we had the pack train ready. Edd and Doyle climbed on the wagon to start the other way. Romer waved his hand: "Good-bye, Mr. Doyle, don't break down and lose the apples!"

Then we were off, up the narrow trail along the creek. Haught led the way. Romer attached himself to the bear-

hunter, and wherever the trail was wide enough rode beside
him. R. C. and I followed. The other men fell in behind the
pack train.

The ride was hot, and for the most part all up hill. That
basin could be likened to the ribs of a washboard: it was all
hills, gorges, ridges and ravines. The hollows of this exceedingly rough country were thick with pine and oak, the ridges
covered with cedar, juniper, and manzanita. The ground,
where it was not rocky, was a dry, red clay. We passed
Haught's log cabin and clearing of a few acres, where I saw
fat hogs and cattle. Beyond this point the trail grew more
zigzag, and steeper, and shadier. As we got higher up the air
grew cooler. I noted a change in the timber. The trees grew
larger, and other varieties appeared. We crossed a roaring
brook lined by thick, green brush, very pleasant to the eye,
and bronze-gold ferns that were beautiful. We passed oaks all
green and yellow, and maple trees, wonderfully colored red
and cerise. Then still higher up I espied some silver spruces,
most exquisite trees of the mountain forests.

During the latter half of the climb up to the rim I had to
attend to the business of riding and walking. The trail was
rough, steep, and long. Once Haught called my attention to a
flat stone with a plain trail made by a turtle in ages past when
that sandstone was wet, sedimentary deposit. By and bye we
reached the last slopes up to the mesa, green, with yellow
crags and cliffs, and here and there blazing maples to remind
me again that autumn was at hand.

At last we surmounted the rim, from which I saw a scene
that defied words. It was different from any I had seen
before. Black timber as far as eye could see! Then I saw a
vast bowl inclosed by dim mountain ranges, with a rolling
floor of forested ridges, and dark lines I knew to be canyons.
For wild, rugged beauty I had not seen its equal.

When the pack train reached the rim we rode on, and now
through a magnificent forest at eight thousand feet altitude.
Big white and black clouds obscured the sun. A thunder shower
caught us. There was hail, and the dry smell of dust, and a
little cold rain. Romer would not put on his slicker. Haught
said the drought had been the worst he had seen in twenty

years there. Up in this odorous forestland I could not see where there had been lack of rain. The forest appeared thick, grassy, gold and yellow and green and brown. Thickets and swales of oaks and aspens were gorgeous in their autumn hues. The silver spruces sent down long, graceful branches that had to be brushed aside or stooped under as we rode along. Big gray squirrels with white tails and tufted ears ran up trees to perch on limbs and watch us go by; and other squirrels, much smaller and darker gray, frisked and chattered and scolded at a great rate.

We passed little depressions that ran down into ravines, and these, Haught informed me, were the heads of canyons that sloped away from the rim, deepening and widening for miles. The rim of the mesa was its highest point, except here and there a few elevations like Black Butte. Geologically this mesa was an enormous fault, like the north rim of the Grand Canyon. During the formation of the earth, or the hardening of the crust, there had been a crack or slip, so that one edge of the crust stood up sheer above the other. We passed the heads of Leonard Canyon, Gentry, and Turkey Canyons, and at last, near time of sunset, headed down into beautifully colored, pine-sloped, aspen-thicketed Beaver Dam Canyon.

A mile from the rim we were deep in the canyon, walled in by rock-strewn and pine-timbered slopes too steep for a horse to climb. There was a little gully on the black soil where there were no evidences of recent water. Haught said he had never seen Beaver Dam Creek dry until this season. We traveled on until we came to a wide, open space, where three forks of this canyon met, and where in the middle of this glade there rose a lengthy wooded bench, shaded and beautified by stately pines and silver spruce. At this point water appeared in the creek bed, flowing in tiny stream that soon gathered volume. Cold and clear and pure it was all that was needed to make this spot an ideal camp site. Haught said half a mile below there was a grassy park where the horses would graze with elk.

We pitched our tents on this bench, and I chose for my location a space between two great monarchs of the forests, that had surely shaded many an Indian encampment. At the upper end of the bench rose a knoll, golden and green with scrub oaks, and russet-colored with its lichened rocks. About all we could manage that evening was to eat and go to bed.

Morning broke cool and bright, with heavy dew. I got my boots as wet as if I had waded in water. This surprised me, occurring on October sixth, and at eight thousand feet altitude, as I had expected frost. Most of this day was spent in making camp, unpacking, and attending to the many necessary little details that make for comfort in the open. To be sure Romer worked very spasmodically. He spent most of his time on the back of one of Haught's burros, chasing and roping another. I had not remembered seeing the lad so happily occupied.

Late in the afternoon I slipped off down the canyon alone, taking Haught's rifle for safety rather than a desire to kill anything. By no means was it impossible to meet a bad bear in that forest. Some distance below camp I entered a ravine and climbed up to the level, and soon found myself deep in the fragrant, colorful, wild forest. Like coming home again was it to enter that forest of silver-tipped, level-spreading spruce, and great, gnarled, massive pines, and oak-patches of green and gold, and maple thickets, with shining aspens standing white against the blaze of red and purple. High, wavy, bleached grass, brown mats of pine needles, gray-green moss waving from the spruces, long strands of sunlight—all these seemed to welcome me.

At a distance there was a roar of wind through the forest; close at hand only a soft breeze. Rustling of twigs caused me to compose myself to listen and watch. Soon small gray squirrels came into view all around me, bright-eyed and saucy, very curious about this intruder. They began to chatter. Other squirrels were working in the tops of trees, for I heard the fall of pine cones. Then came the screech of blue jays. Soon they too discovered me. The male birds were superb, dignified, beautiful. The color was light blue all over with dark blue head and tufted crest. By and bye they ceased to scold me, and I was left to listen to the wind, and to the tiny patter of dropping seeds and needles from the spruces. What cool, sweet, fresh smell this woody, leafy, earthy, dry, grassy, odorous fragrance, dominated by scent of pine! How lonesome and restful! I felt a sense of deep peace and rest. This golden-green forest, barred with sunlight, canopied by the blue sky, and melodious with its soughing moan of wind, absolutely filled me with content and happiness. If a stag or a bear had trotted out into my sight, and had showed me no animosity, not improbably I would have forgotten my gun. More and more as I lived in the open I grew reluctant to kill.

Presently a porcupine waddled along some rods away, and unaware of my presence it passed by and climbed a spruce. I saw it climb high and finally lost sight of it. In searching up and down this spruce I grew alive to what a splendid and beautiful tree it was. Where so many trees grew it always seemed difficult to single out one and study it. This silver spruce was five feet through at the base, rugged, gray-seamed, thick all the way to its lofty height. Its branches were small, with a singular feature that they were uniform in shape, length, and droop. Most all spruce branches drooped toward the ground. That explained why they made such excellent shelters from rain. After a hard storm I had seen the ground dry under a thick-foliaged spruce. Many a time had I made a bed under one. Elk and deer stand under a spruce during a rain, unless there is thunder and lightning. In forests of high altitude, where lightning strikes many trees, I have never found or heard of elk and deer being killed. This particular spruce was a natural tent in the forest. The thick-spreading graceful silver plumes extended clear to the top, where they were bushiest, and rounded out, with all the largest branches there. Each dark gray branch was fringed and festooned with pale green moss, like the cypresses of the South.

Suddenly I heard a sharp snapping of twigs and then stealthy, light steps. An animal of some species was moving in the thicket nearby. Naturally I sustained a thrill, and bethought me of the rifle. Then I peered keenly into the red rose shadows of the thicket. The sun was setting now, and though there appeared a clear golden light high in the forest, along the ground there were shadows. I heard leaves falling, rustling. Tall white aspens stood out of the thicket, and two of the large ones bore the old black scars of bear claws. I was

sure, however, that no bear hid in the thicket at this moment.
Presently whatever the animal was it pattered lightly away on
the far side. After that I watched the quiver of the aspen
leaves. Some were green, some yellow, some gold, but they
all had the same wonderful tremor, the silent fluttering that
gave them the most exquisite action in nature. The sun set,
the forest darkened, reminding me of supper time. So I
returned to camp. As I entered the open canyon Romer-boy
espied me—manifestly he had been watching—and he yelled:
"Here comes my Daddy now! . . . Say, Dad, did you get any
pegs?"

Next morning Haught asked me if I would like to ride
around through the woods and probably get a shot at a deer.
Romer coaxed so to go that I finally consented.

We rode down the canyon, and presently came to a wide
grassy park inclosed by high green-clad slopes, the features of
which appeared to be that the timber on the west slope was
mostly pine, and on the east slope it was mostly spruce. I
could arrive at no certain reason for this, but I thought it must
be owing to the snow lying somewhat longer on the east
slope. The stream here was running with quite a little volume
of water. Our horses were grazing in this park. I saw fresh elk
tracks made the day before. Elk were quite abundant through
this forest, Haught informed me, and were protected by law.

A couple of miles down this trail the canyon narrowed,
losing its park-like dimensions. The farther we traveled the
more water there was in the stream, and more elk, deer, and
turkey tracks in the sand. Every half mile or so we would
come to the mouth of a small intersecting canyon, and at
length we rode up one of these, presently to climb out on top.
At this distance from the rim the forest was more open than in
the vicinity of our camp, affording better riding and hunting.
Still the thickets of aspen and young pine were so frequent
that seldom could I see ahead more than several hundred
yards.

Haught led the way, I rode next and Romer kept beside me
where it was possible to do so. There was, however, no trail.
How difficult to keep the lad quiet! I expected of course that
Haught would dismount, and take me to hunt on foot. After a

while I gathered he did not hunt deer except on horseback. He explained that cowboys rounded up cattle in this forest in the spring and fall, and deer were not frightened at sound or sight of a horse. Some of the thrill and interest in the forest subsided for me. I did not like to hunt in a country where cattle ranged, no matter how wild they were. Then when we came to a forested ridge bare of grass and smelling of sheep, that robbed the forest of a little more glamour. Mexican sheep-herders drove their flocks up this far sometimes. Haught said bear, lion, lynx, and coyote, sometimes the big gray wolves, followed the sheep. Deer, however, hated a sheep-run range.

Riding was exceedingly pleasant. The forest was shady, cool, full of sunlight and beauty. Nothing but fire or the lumbermen could ever rob it of its beauty, silence, fragrance, and of its temple-like majesty. So provided we did not meet any cattle or sheep I did not care whether or not we sighted any game. In fact I would have forgotten we were hunting had not Romer been along. With him continually seeing things it was difficult to keep from imagining that we were hunting Indians. The Apaches had once lived in this country Haught informed us; and it was a habit of theirs to burn the grass and fallen leaves over every fall, thus keeping down the underbrush. In this the Indians showed how near-sighted they were; the future growth of a forest did not concern them. Usually Indians were better conservationists than white men.

We rode across a grove of widely separated, stately pines, at the far end of which stood a thicket of young pines and other brush. As we neared this Haught suddenly reined in, and in quick and noiseless action he dismounted. Then he jerked his rifle from his saddlesheath, took a couple of forward steps, and leveled it. I was so struck with the rugged and significant picture he made that I did not dismount, and did not see any game until after he fired. Then as I tumbled off and got out my rifle I heard Romer gasping and crying out. A gray streak with a bobbing white end flashed away out of sight to the left. Next I saw a deer bounding through the thicket. Haught fired again. The deer ran so fast that I could not get my sights anywhere near him. Haught thudded through an opening, and an instant later, when both he and the deer had disappeared, he shot the third time. Presently he returned.

"Never could shoot with them open sights nohow," he said. "Shore I missed thet yearlin' buck when he was standin'. Why didn't you smoke him up?"

"Dad, why didn't you peg him?" asked Romer, with intense regret. "Why, I could have knocked him."

Then it was incumbent upon me to confess that the action had appeared to be a little swift. "Wal," said Haught, "when you see one you want to pile off quick."

As we rode on Romer naively asked me if ever in my life I had seen anything run so fast as that deer. We entered another big grove with thin patches of thicket here and there. Haught said these were good places for deer to lie down, relying on their noses to scent danger from windward, and on their eyes in the other direction. We circled to go round thickets, descending somewhat into a swale. Here Haught got off a little to the right. Romer and I rode up a gentle slope toward a thin line of little pines, through which I could see into the pines beyond. Suddenly up jumped three big gray bucks. Literally I fell off my horse, bounced up, and pulled out my rifle. One buck was loping in a thicket. I could see his broad, gray body behind the slender trees. I aimed—followed him—got a bead on him—and was just about to pull trigger when he vanished. Plunging forward I yelled to Haught. Then Romer cried in his shrill treble: "Dad, here's a big buck—hurry!" Turning I ran back. In wild excitement Romer was pointing. I was just in time to see a gray rump disappear in the green. Just then Haught shot, and after that he halloed. Romer and I went through the thicket, working to our left, and presently came out into the open forest. Haught was leading his horse. To Romer's eager query he replied: "Shore, I piled him up. Two-year-old black-tail buck."

Sure enough he had shot straight this time. The buck lay motionless under a pine, with one point of his antlers imbedded deep in the ground. A sleek, gray, graceful deer he was just beginning to get his winter coat. His color was indeed a bluish gray. Haught hung him up to a branch, spread his hind legs, and cut him down the middle. The hunter's dexterity

with a knife made me wonder how many deer he had dressed
in his life in the open. We lifted the deer upon the saddle of
Haught's horse and securely tied it there with a lasso; then
with the hunter on foot, leading the way, we rode through the
forest up the main ridge between Beaver and Turkey Canyons. Toward the rim I found the pines and spruces larger,
and the thickets of aspen denser. We passed the heads of
many ravines running down to the canyons on either side, and
these were blazing gold and red in color, and so thick I could
not see a rod into them. About the middle of the afternoon we
reached camp. With venison hanging up to cool we felt
somewhat like real hunters. R. C. had gone off to look for
turkeys, which enterprise had been unsuccessful.

Upon the following day, which was October tenth, we
started our bear hunting. Haught's method appeared to me to
lack something. He sent the hounds down below the rim with
George; and taking R. C. and me, and Lee and Nielsen, he
led us over to what he called Horton Thicket. Never would I
forget my first sight of that immense forest-choked canyon. It
was a great cove running up from the basin into the rim.
Craggy ledges, broken, ruined, tottering and gray, slanted
down into this abyss. The place was so vast that these ledges
appeared far apart, yet they were many. An empire of splintered cliff!

High up these cracked and stained walls were covered with
lichens, with little spruces growing in niches, and tiny yellow
bushes. Points of crumbling rock were stained gold and russet
and bronze. Below the huge gorge was full of aspens, maples, spruces—a green, crimson, yellow density of timber,
apparently impenetrable. We were accorded different stations
on the ledges all around the cove, and instructed to stay there
until called by four blasts from a hunting horn. My point was
so far from R. C.'s, across the canyon, that I had to use my
field-glass to see him. When I did look he seemed contented.
Lee and Nielsen and Haught I could not see at all. Finding a
comfortable seat, if hard rock could ever be that, I proceeded
to accept my wait for developments. One thing was sure—
even though it were a futile way to hunt it seemed rich in
other recompense for me. My stand towered above a vast

colorful slope down which the wind roared as in a gale. How could I ever hear the hounds? I watched the storm-clouds scudding across the sky. Once I saw a rare bird, a black eagle in magnificent flight; and so whatever happened I had my reward in that sight.

Nothing happened. For hours and hours I sat there, with frequent intermissions away from my hard, rocky seat. Toward the close of afternoon, when the wind began to get cold, I saw that R. C. had left his stand. He had undoubtedly gone back to camp, which was some miles nearer his stand than mine. At last I gave up any hope of hearing either the hounds or the horn, as the roar of wind had increased. Once I thought I heard a distant rifle shot. So I got on my horse and set out to find camp. I was on a promontory, the sides of which were indented by long ravines that were impassable except near their heads. In fact I had been told there was only one narrow space where it was possible to get off this promontory. Lucky indeed that I remembered Haught telling of this! Anyway I soon found myself lost in a maze of forested heads of ravines. Finally I went back to the rim on the west side, and then working along I found our horse-tracks. These I followed, with difficulty, and after an hour's travel I crossed the narrow neck of the promontory, and back-tracked myself to camp, arriving there at sunset.

The Haughts had put up two bear. One bear had worked around under one of the great promontories. The hounds had gotten on his back-trail, staying on it until it grew cold, then had left it. Their baying had roused the bear out of his bed, and he had showed himself once or twice on the open rock-slides. Haught saw the other bear from the rim. This was a big, red, cinnamon bear asleep under a pine tree on an open slope. Haught said when the hounds gave tongue on the other trail this red bear awakened, sat up, and wagged his head slowly. He had never been chased by hounds. He lay down in his piny bed again. The distance was too great for an accurate shot, but Haught tried anyway, with the result that he at least scared the cinnamon off.

These bear were both thin. As they were not the sheep-killing and cow-killing kind their food consisted mainly of

mast (acorns) and berries. But this season there were no
berries at all, and very few acorns. So the bears were not fat.
When a bear was thin he could always outrun the hounds; if
he was fat he would get hot and tired enough to climb a tree
or mad enough to stop and fight the dogs.

Haught told me there were a good many mountain lions
and lynx under the rim. They lived on elk, deer, and turkey.
The lynx were the tuft-eared, short-tailed species. They would
attack and kill a cow-elk. In winter on the rim the snow
sometimes fell fifteen feet deep, so that the game wintered
underneath. Snow did not lay long on the sunny, open ridges
of the basin.

That night a storm-wind roared mightily in the pines. How
wonderful to lie snug in bed, down in the protected canyon,
and hear the marching and retreating gale above in the forest!
Next day we expected rain or snow. But there was only wind,
and that quieted by afternoon. So I took Romer off into the
woods. He carried his rifle and he wore his chaps. I could not
persuade him to part with these. They rustled on the brush
and impeded his movements, and particularly tired him, and
made him look like a diminutive cowboy. How eager, keen,
boyishly vain, imaginative! He was crazy to see game, to
shoot anything, particularly bears. But it contented him to
hunt turkeys. Many a stump and bit of color he mistook for
game of some kind. Nevertheless, I had to take credence in
what he thought he saw, for his eyesight was unusually quick
and keen.

That afternoon Edd and Doyle arrived, reporting an extremely rough, roundabout climb up to the rim, where they
had left the wagon. As it was impossible to haul the supplies
down into the canyon they were packed down to camp on
burros. Isbel had disapproved of this procedure, a circumstance that struck me with peculiar significance, which Lee
explained by telling me Isbel was one of the peculiar breed of
cowboys, who no sooner were they out on the range than they
wanted to go back to town again. The truth was I had not met
any of that breed, though I had heard of them. This peculiar-
ity of Isbel's began to be related in my mind to his wastefulness
as a cook. He cooked and threw away as much as we ate. I

asked him to be careful and to go easy with our supplies, but I could not see that my request made any difference.

After supper this evening R. C. heard a turkey call up on the hill east of camp. Then I heard it, and Romer also. We ran out a ways into the open to listen the better. R. C.'s ears were exceptionally keen. He could hear a squirrel jump a long distance in the forest. In this case he distinctly heard three turkeys fly up into trees. I heard one. Romer declared he heard a flock. Then R. C. located a big bronze and white gobbler on a lower limb of a huge pine. Presently I too espied it. Whereupon we took shot-gun and rifle, and sallied forth sure of fetching back to camp some wild turkey meat. Romer tagged at our heels.

Hurrying to the slope we climbed up at least three-quarters of the way, as swiftly as possible. And that was work enough to make me wet and hot. The sun had set and twilight was upon us, so that we needs must hurry if we were to be successful. Locating the big gobbler turned out to be a task. We had to climb over brush and around rocks, up a steep slope, rather open; and we had to do it without being seen or making noise. Romer, despite his eagerness, did very well indeed. At last I espied our quarry, and indeed the sight was thrilling. Wild turkey gobblers to me, who had hunted them enough to learn how sagacious and cunning and difficult to stalk they were, always seemed as provocative of excitement as larger game. This big fellow hopped up from limb to limb of the huge dead pine, and he bobbed around as if undecided, and tried each limb for a place to roost. Then he hopped farther up until we lost sight of him in the gnarled net-work of branches.

R. C. wanted me to slip on alone, but I preferred to have him and Romer go too. So we slipped stealthily upward until we reached the level. Then progress was easier. I went to the left with the rifle, and R. C. with the .20-gauge, and Romer, went around to the right. How rapidly it was growing dark! Low down in the forest I could not distinguish objects. We circled that big pine tree, and I made rather a wide detour, perhaps eighty yards from it. At last I got the upper part of the dead pine silhouetted against the western sky. Moving to and fro I finally made out a large black lump way out upon a spreading branch. Could that be the gobbler? I studied that dark enlarged part of the limb with great intentness, and I had about decided that it was only a knot when I saw a long neck shoot out. That lump was the wise old turkey all right. He was almost in the top of the tree and far out from the trunk. No wild cat or lynx could ever surprise him there! I reflected upon the instinct that governed him to protect his life so cunningly. Safe he was from all but man and gun!

When I came to aim at him with the rifle I found that I could see only a blur of sights. Other branches and the tip of a very high pine adjoining made a dark background. I changed my position, working around to where the background was all open sky. It proved to be better. By putting the sights against this open sky I could faintly see the front sight through the blurred ring. It was a good long shot even for daylight, and I had a rifle I knew nothing about. But all the difficulty only made a keener zest. Just then I heard Romer cry out excitedly, and then R. C. spoke distinctly. Far more careless than that they began to break twigs under their feet. The gobbler grew uneasy. How he stretched out his long neck! He heard them below. I called out low and sharp: "Stand still! Be quiet!" Then I looked again through the blurred peep-sight until I caught the front sight against the open sky. This done I moved the rifle over until I had the sight aligned against the dark shape. Straining my eyes I held hard—then fired. The big dark lump on the branch changed shape, and fell, to alight with a sounding thump. I heard Romer running, but could not see him. Then his high voice pealed out: "I got him, Dad. You made a grand peg!"

Not only had Romer gotten him, but he insisted on packing him back to camp. The gobbler was the largest I ever killed, not indeed one of the huge thirty-five pounders, but a fat, heavy turkey, and quite a load for a boy. Romer packed him down that steep slope in the dark without a slip, for which performance I allowed him to stay up a while around the camp-fire.

The Haughts came over from their camp that night and visited us. Much as I loved to sit alone beside a red-embered

fire at night in the forest, or on the desert, I also liked upon
occasions to have company. We talked and talked. Old-timer
Doyle told more than one of his "in the early days" stories.
Then Haught told us some bear stories. The first was about an
old black bear charging and sliding down at him. He said no
hunter should ever shoot at a bear above him, because it
could come down at him as swiftly as a rolling rock. This
time he worked the lever of his rifle at lightning speed, and at
the last shot he "shore saw bar hair right before his eyes."
His second story was about a boy who killed a bear, and was
skinning it when five more bears came along, in single file,
and made it very necessary that he climb a tree until they had
gone. His third story was about an old she-bear that had two
cubs. Haught happened to ride within sight of her when
evidently she thought it time to put her cubs in a safe place.
So she tried to get them to climb a spruce tree, and finally
had to cuff and spank them to make them go up. In connec-
tion with this story he told us he had often seen she-bears
spank their cubs. More thrilling was his fourth story about a
huge grizzly, a sheep and cattle killer that passed through the
country, leaving death behind him on the range.

Romer's enjoyment of this story-telling hour around the
glowing camp-fire was equalled by his reluctance to go to
bed. "Aw, Dad, please let me hear one more," he pleaded.
His shining eyes would have weakened a sterner discipline
than mine. And Haught seemed inspired by them.

"Wal now, listen to this hyar," he began again, with a
twinkle in his eye. "Thar was an old fellar had a ranch in
Chevelon Canyon, an' he was always bein' pestered by mountain lions. His name was Bill Tinker. Now Bill was no sort of
a hunter, fact was he was afeerd of lions an' bears, but he
shore did git riled when any critters rustled around his cabin.
One day in the fall he comes home an' seen a big she-lion
sneakin' around. He grabbed a club, an' throwed it, and
yelled to scare the critter away. Wal, he had an old water
barrel layin' around, an' darned if the lion didn't run in thet
barrel an' hide. Bill run quick an' flopped the barrel end up,
so he had the lion trapped. He had to set on the barrel to hold
it down. Shore that lion raised old Jasper under the barrel.

Bill was plumb scared. Then he seen the lion's tail stick out through the bung-hole. Bill bent over an' shore quick tied a knot in thet long tail. Then he run fer his cabin. When he got to the door he looked back to see the lion tearin' down the hill fer the woods with the barrel bumpin, behind her. Bill said he never seen her again till next spring, an' she had the barrel still on her tail. But what was stranger'n thet Bill swore she had four cubs with her an' each of them had a keg on its tail.''

We all roared with laughter except Romer. His interest had been so all-absorbing, his excitement so great, and his faith in the story-teller so reverential that at first he could not grasp the trick at the end of the story. His face was radiant, his eyes were dark and dilated. When the truth dawned upon him, amaze and disappointment changed his mobile face, and then came mirth. He shouted as if to the tree-tops on high. Long after he was in bed I heard him laughing to himself.

I was awakened a little after daylight by the lad trying to get into his boots. His boots were rather tight, and somehow, even in a dry forest, he always contrived to get them wet, so that in the morning it was a Herculean task for him to pull them on. This occasion appeared more strenuous than usual. "Son, what's the idea?" I inquired. "It's just daylight—not time to get up." He desisted from his labors long enough to pant: "Uncle Rome's—gone after turkeys. Edd's going to—call them with—a caller—made out of a turkey's wing-bone." And I said: "But they've gone now." Whereupon he subsided: "Darned old boots! I heard Edd and Uncle Rome. I'd been ready if I could have got into my darned old boots. . . . See here, Dad, I'm gonna wear moccasins."

III

As we were sitting round the camp-fire, eating breakfast, R. C. and Edd retured; and R. C. carried a turkey gobbler the very size and color of the one I had shot the night before. R. C.'s face wore the keen, pleased expression characteristic of it when he had just had some unusual and satisfying experience. "Sure was great," he said, warming his hands at the fire.

"We went up on the hill where you killed your gobbler last night. Got there just in the gray light of dawn. We were careful not to make any noise. Edd said if there were any more turkeys they would come down at daylight. So we waited until it was light enough to see. Then Edd got out his turkey bone and began to call. Turkeys answered from the trees all around. By George, it was immense! Edd had picked out a thicket of little pines for us to hide in, and in front of us was a glade with a big fallen tree lying across it. Edd waited a few moments. The woods was all gray and quiet. I don't know when I've felt so good. Then he called again. At once turkeys answered from all around in the trees. Next I heard a swish of wings, then a thump. Then more swishes. The turkeys were flying down from their roosts. It seemed to me in my excitement that there were a hundred of them. We could hear them pattering over the dry ground. Edd whispered: 'They're down. Now we got to do some real callin'.' I felt how tense, how cautious he was. When he called again there was some little difference, I don't know what, unless it was his call sounded more like a real turkey. They answered. They were gathering in front of us, and I made sure were coming into the glade. Edd stopped calling. Then he whispered: 'Ready now. Look out!' . . . Sure I was looking all right. This was my first experience calling turkeys and I simply shook all over. Suddenly I saw a turkey head stick up over the log. Then!—up hopped a beautiful gobbler. He walked along the log, looked and peered, and stretched his neck. Sure he was suspicious. Edd gave me a hunch, which I took to be a warning to shoot quick. That was a hard place for me. I wanted to watch the gobbler. I wanted to see the others. We could hear them all over the glade. But this was my chance. Quickly I rose and took a peg at him. A cloud of feathers puffed off him. He gave a great bounce, flapping his wings. I heard a roaring whirr of other turkeys. With my eye on my gobbler I seemed to see the air full of big, black, flying things. My gobbler came down, bounced up again, got going—when with the second barrel I knocked him cold. Then I stood there watching the flock whirring every way into the forest. Must have been thirty-five or forty of them, all gobblers. It was a great sight. And right here I declared myself—wild turkey is the game for me.''

Romer manifestly listened to this narrative with mingled feelings of delight and despair. ''Uncle Rome, wild turkey's the game for me, too . . . and by Gosh! I'll fix those boots of mine!''

That morning we were scheduled for another bear hunt, on which I had decided to go down under the rim with Edd and George. Lee had his doubts about my horse, and desired me to take his, or at least one of the others. Now his horse was too spirited for me to ride after hounds, and I did not want to take one of the others, so I was compelled to ride my own. At the last moment Lee had been disappointed in getting a mustang he particularly wanted for me, and so it had fallen about that my horse was the poorest in the outfit, which to put it mildly was pretty poor. I had made the best of the matter so far, and hoped to continue doing so.

We rode up the east slope of Beaver Dam Canyon, through the forest, and out along the rim for five or six miles, way on the other side of the promontory where I had gotten lost. Here Haught left us, taking with him R. C. and Lee and Nielsen, all of whom were to have stands along the rim. We hoped to start a bear and chase him round under the high points toward Horton Thicket.

The magnificent view from the head of a trail where Edd started down impressed me so powerfully that I lagged behind. Below me heaved a split, tossed, dimpled, waving, rolling world of black-green forestland. Far across it stood up a rugged, blue, waved range of mountains—the Sierra Anchas.

The trail was rough, even for Arizonians, which made it for me little short of impassable. I got off to lead my horse. He had to be pulled most of the time, wherefore I lost patience with him. I loved horses, but not stubborn ones. All the way down the rocky trail the bunch grass and wild oak and manzanita were so thick that I had to crush my way through. At length I had descended the steep part to find Edd and George waiting for me below on the juniper benches. These were slopes of red earth or clay, bare of grass, but thick with junipers, cactus, and manzanita. This face of the great rim was a southern exposure, hot and dusty. The junipers were thick. The green of their foliage somewhat resembled cedars, but their berries were gray-blue, almost lavender in color. I tasted several from different trees, until I found one with sweet, somewhat acrid taste. Significant it was that this juniper had broken branches where bears had climbed to eat the fruit, and all around on the ground beneath was bear sign. Edd said the tracks were cold, but all the same he had to be harsh with the hounds to hold them in. I counted twenty piles of bear manure under one juniper, and many places where bears had scraped in the soft earth and needles.

We went on down this slope, getting into thicker brush and rougher ground. All at once the hounds opened up in thrilling chorus of bays and barks. I saw Edd jump off his horse to stoop and examine the ground, where evidently he had seen a bear track. "Fresh—made last night!" he yelled, mounting hurriedly. "Hi! Hi! Hi!" His horse leaped through the brush, and George followed. In an instant they were out of sight. Right there my trouble began. I spurred my horse after them, and it developed that he differed from me in regard to direction and going. He hated the brush. But I made him take to it and made him run. Dodging branches was an old story for me, and if I had been on a good fast horse I might have kept Edd and George in sight. As it was, however, I had to follow them by the sound of hoofs and breaking brush. From the way the hounds bayed I knew they had struck a hot scent. They worked down the slope, and assuredly gave me a wild ride to keep within hearing of them. My horse grew excited, which fact increased his pace, his obstinacy, and likewise my danger. Twice he unseated me. I tore my coat, lost my hat, scratched my face, skinned my knees, but somehow I managed to keep within hearing.

I came to a deep brush-choked gorge, impassable at that point. Luckily the hounds turned here and started back my way. By riding along the edge of this gorge I kept up with them. They climbed out an intersecting ravine and up on the opposite side. I forced my horse to go down this rather steep soft slope. At the bottom I saw a little spring of water with fresh bear tracks around it, and one place where the bear had caved in a soft bank. Here my horse suddenly plunged and went to his knees in the yielding red clay. He snorted in fright. The bank slid with him and I tumbled off. But nothing serious happened. I ran down, caught him, mounted, and spurred him up the other side. Once up he began to run. I heard the boys yelling not far away and the hounds were baying up above me. They were climbing fast, working to the left, toward an oak thicket. It took effort to slow down my steed. He acted crazy and I began to suspect that he had caught a whiff of the bear. Most horses are afraid of bears and lions. Sight of Edd and George, who appeared in an open spot, somewhat quieted my mount.

"Trail's gettin' hot up there," declared Edd. "That bear's bedded somewhere an' I'll bet the hounds jumped him. Listen to Old Tom!"

How the deep sonorous bay of Old Tom awoke the echoes under the cliffs! And Old Dan's voice was a hoarse bellow. The other hounds yelped.

Edd blew a mellow blast from his hunting-horn, and that awoke other and more melodious echoes. "There's father up on the rim," he said. I looked, and finally saw Haught perched like a black eagle on a crag. His gun flashed in the strong sunlight.

Somewhere up there the hounds jumped the bear. Anybody could have told that. What a wild chorus! Edd and George answered to it with whoops as wild, and they galloped their horses over ground and through brush where they should have been walked. I followed, or tried to follow; and here my steed showed his bullheaded, obstinate nature. If he had been afraid but still game I would have respected him, but he was a coward and mean. He wanted to have his way, which was to go the other direction, and to rid himself of me. So we had it hot and heavy along that rough slope, with honors about even. As for bruises and scratches, however, I sustained the most. In the excitement of the chase and anger at the horse I forgot all about any risks. This always is the way in adventure. Hot racing blood governed me entirely. Whenever I got out in an open place, where I could ride fast and hear and see, then it was all intensely thrilling. Both hounds and comrades were above me, but apparently working down.

Thus for me the necessity of hurry somewhat lessened. I slowed to a trot, peering everywhere, listening with all my ears. I had stopped yelling, because my horse had misunderstood that. We got into a region of oak thickets, small saplings, scrubby, close together, but beautiful with their autumn-tinted leaves. Next I rode through a maple dell, shady, cool, where the leafy floor was all rose-pink-red. My horse sent the colored leaves flying.

Soon, however, we got into the thickets again, low liveoak and manzanita, which kind of brush my horse detested. I did not blame him for that. As the hounds began to work down my keen excitement increased. If they had jumped the bear and were chasing him down I might run upon him any moment. This both appealed to me and caused me apprehension. Suppose he were a bad cinnamon or a grizzly? What would become of me on that horse? I decided that I had better carry my rifle in my hand, so in case of a sudden appearance of the bear and I was thrown or had a fall off, then I would be prepared. So forthwith I drew the rifle out of the scabbard, remembering as I did so that Haught had cautioned me, in case of close quarters with a bear and the need of quick shooting, to jerk the lever down hard. If my horse had cut up abominably before he now began to cover himself with a glory of abominableness. I had to jam him through the thickets. He was an uncomfortable horse to ride under the best circumstances; here he was as bad as riding a picket-fence. When he got his head, which was often, he carried me into thickets of manzanita that we could not penetrate, and had to turn back. I found that I was working high up the slope, and bad luck as I was having with my horse, I still appeared to keep fairly close to the hounds.

When we topped a ridge of this slope the wind struck us strong in the face. The baying of the hounds rang clear and full and fierce. My horse stood straight up. Then he plunged back and bolted down the slope. His mouth was like iron. I could neither hold nor turn him. However perilous this ride I had to admit that at last my horse was running beautifully. In fact he was running away! He had gotten a hot scent of that bear. He hurdled rocks, leaped washes, slid down banks, plunged over places that made my hair stand up stiff, and worst of all he did not try to avoid brush or trees or cactus. Manzanita he tore right through, leaving my coat in strips decorating our wake. I had to hold on, to lie flat, to dodge and twist, and all the time watch for a place where I might fall off in safety. But I did not get a chance to fall off. A loud clamoring burst from the hounds apparently close behind drove my horse frantic. Before he had only run—now he flew! He left me hanging in the thick branches of a juniper, from which I dropped blind and breathless and stunned. Disengaging myself from the broken and hanging branches I staggered aside, rifle in hand, trying to recover breath and wits.

Then, in that nerveless and shaken condition, I heard the breaking of twigs and thud of soft steps right above me. Peering up with my half-blinded eyes I saw a huge red furry animal coming, half obscured by brush. It waved aside from his broad back. A shock ran over me—a bursting gush of hot blood that turned to ice as it rushed. "Big cinnamon bear!" I whispered, hoarsely.

Instinctively I cocked and leveled the rifle, and though I could not clearly see the red animal bearing down the slope, such was my state that I fired. Then followed a roaring crash—a terrible breaking onslaught upon the brush—and the huge red mass seemed to flash down toward me. I worked the lever of the rifle. But I had forgotten Haught's caution. I did not work the lever far enough down, so that the next cartridge jarnmed in the receiver. With a second shock, different this time, I tried again. In vain! The terrible crashing of brush appeared right upon me. For an instant that seemed an age I stood riveted to the spot, my blood congealing, my heart choking me, my tongue pasted to the roof of my mouth. Then I dropped the rifle and whirled to plunge away. Like a deer I bounded. I took prodigious bounds. To escape—to find a tree to leap into—that was my only thought. A few rods down the slope—it seemed a mile—I reached a pine with low branches. Like a squirrel I ran up this—straddled a limb high up—and gazed back.

My sensations then were dominated by the relief of salvation. I became conscious of them. Racing blood, bursting heart, labored pang of chest, prickling, burning skin, a queer involuntary flutter of muscles, like a palsy—these attested to the instinctive primitive nature of my state. I heard the crashing of brush, the pound of soft jumps over to my left. With eyes that seemed magnifying I gazed to see a big red woolly steer plunge wildly down the slope and disappear. A third shock possessed me—amaze. I had mistaken a wild, frightened steer for a red cinnamon bear!

I sat there some moments straddling that branch. Then I descended, and went back to the place I had dropped my rifle, and securing that I stood a moment listening. The hounds had taken the chase around below me into the gorge and were drawing away. It was useless to try to follow them. I sat down again and gave myself up to meditation.

I tried to treat the situation as a huge joke, but that would not go. No joke indeed! My horse had made me risk too much, my excitement had been too intense, my fright had been too terrible. Reality for me could not have been any more grave. I had risked my neck on a stubborn coward of a horse, I had mistaken a steer for a bear, I had forgotten how to manipulate the borrowed rifle. These were the careless elements of tragedy. The thought sobered me. I took the lesson to heart. And I reflected on the possible point of view of the bear. He had probably gone to sleep on a full stomach of juniper berries and a big drink of spring water. Rudely he had been routed out by a pack of yelping, fiendish hounds. He had to run for his life. What had he done to deserve such treatment? Possibly he might have killed some of Haught's pigs, but most assuredly he had never harmed me. In my sober frame of mind then I rather disapproved of my wholly unjustifiable murderous intent. I would have deserved it if the steer had really been the bear. Certainly I hoped the bear would outrun the hounds and escape. I weighed the wonderful thrill of the chase, the melody of hounds, the zest of spirited action, the peril to limb and life against the thing that they were done for, with the result that I found them sadly lacking. Peril to limb and life was good for man. If this had not been a fact my performance would have been as cowardly as that of

my horse. Again I had rise up before my mind the spectacle
of opposing forces—the elemental in man restrained by the
spiritual. Then the old haunting thought returned to vex me—
man in his development needed the exercise of brawn, mus-
cle, bone red-blood, violence, labor and pain and agony.
Nature recognized only the survival of the fittest of any
species. If a man allowed a spiritual development, intellect,
gentleness, to keep him from all hard, violent action, from
tremendous exertion, from fierce fight with elements and
beasts, and his own kind—would he not soon degenerate as a
natural physical man? Evolution was a stern inevitable seeking of nature for perfection, for the unattainable. This perfection was something that lived and improved on strife.
Barbarians, Indians, savages were the most perfect specimens
of nature's handiwork; and in proportion to their development
toward so-called civilized life their physical prowess and
perfectness—that was to say, their strength to resist and live
and reproduce their kind—absolutely and inevitably deteriorated.

My reflection did not carry me at that time to any positive
convictions of what was truest and best. The only conclusions
I eventually arrived at were that I was sore and bruised and
dirty and torn—that I would be happy if the bear got away—
that I had lost my mean horse and was glad therefore—that I
would have half a dozen horses and rifles upon my next
hunt—and lastly that I would not be in any hurry to tell about
mistaking a steer for a bear, and climbing a tree. Indeed these
last facts have been religiously kept secret until chronicled here.

Shortly afterward, as I was making a lame and slow head-
way toward Horton Thicket, where I hoped to find a trail out,
I heard Edd yelling, and I answered. Presently we met. He
was leading my horse, and some of the hounds, notably Old
Tom and Dan, were with him.

"Where's the bear?" I asked.

"He got away down in the breaks," replied Edd. "George
is tryin' to call the hounds back. What happened to you? I
heard you shoot."

"My horse didn't care much for me or the brush," I
replied. "He left me—rather suddenly. And—I took a shot at
what I thought was a bear."

"I seen him once," said Edd, with eyes flashing. "Was just goin' to smoke him up when he jumped out of sight."

My mortification and apprehension were somewhat mitigated when I observed that Edd was dirty, ragged, and almost as much disheveled as I was. I had feared he would see in my appearance certain unmistakable evidences that I had made a tenderfoot blunder and then run for my life. But Edd took my loss of hat, and torn coat, and general bedraggled state as a matter of course. Indeed I somehow felt a little pride at his acceptance of me there in the flesh.

We rode around the end of this slope, gradually working down into Horton Thicket, where a wild confusion of dense timber engaged my sight. Presently George trotted up behind us with the other dogs. "We lost him down on the hot dry ridges. Hounds couldn't track him," was all George said. Thereupon Edd blew four blasts upon his hunting-horn, which were signals to those on the stands above that the hunt was over for the day.

Even in the jungle tropics I had never seen such dense shade as this down in Horton Thicket. The timber grew close and large, and the foliage was matted, letting little sunlight through. Dark, green and brown, fragrant, cool thicket indeed it was. We came to a huge spruce tree, the largest I ever saw—Edd said eight feet through at the base, but he was conservative. It was a gnarled, bearded, gray, old monarch of the forest, with bleached, dead top. For many years it had been the home of swarms of wild honey bees. Edd said more than one bee-hunter had undertaken to cut down this spruce. This explained a number of deeply cut notches in the huge trunk. "I'll bet Nielsen could chop it down," declared Edd. I admitted the compliment to our brawny Norwegian axe-wielder, but added that I certainly would not let him do it, whether we were to get any honey or not.

By and bye we reached the bottom of the thicket where we crossed a swift clear cold brook. Here the smells seemed cool, sweet, wild with spruce and pine. This stream of granite water burst from a spring under a cliff. What a roar it made! I drank until I could drink no more. Huge boulders and windfalls, moved by water at flood season, obstructed the narrow stream-bed. We crossed to start climbing the north slope, and soon worked up out of the thicket upon a steep, rocky slope, with isolated pines. We struck a deer-trail hard to follow. Above me loomed the pine-tipped rim, with its crags, cliffs, pinnacles, and walls, all gray, seamed and stained, and in some clefts blazes of deep red and yellow foliage.

When we surmounted the slope, and eventually reached camp, I found Isbel entertaining strangers, men of rough garb, evidently riders of the range. That was all right, but I did not like his prodigality with our swiftly diminishing store of eatables.

To conclude about Isbel—matters pertaining to our commissary department, during the next few days, went from bad to worse. Doyle advised me not to take Isbel to task, and was rather evasive of reasons for so advising me. Of course I listened and attended to my old guide's advice, but I fretted under the restraint. We had a spell of bad weather, wind and rain, and hail off and on, and at length, the third day, a cold drizzling snow. During this spell we did but little hunting. The weather changed, and the day afterward I rode my mean horse twenty miles on a deer hunt. We saw one buck. Upon our arrival at camp, about four o'clock, which hour was too early for dinner, I was surprised and angered to find Isbel eating an elaborate meal with three more strange, rough-appearing men. Doyle looked serious. Nielsen had a sharp glint in his gray eye. As for myself, this procedure of our cook's was more than I could stand.

"Isbel, you're discharged," I said, shortly. "Take your outfit and get out. Lee will lend you a pack horse."

"Wal, I ain't fired," drawled Isbel. "I quit before you rode in. Beat you to it!"

"Then if you quit it seems to me you are taking liberties with supplies you have no right to," I replied.

"Nope. Cook of any outfit has a right to all the chuck he wants. That's western way."

"Isbel, listen to this and then get out," I went on. "You've wasted our supplies just to get us to hurry and break camp. As for western ways I know something of them. It's a western way for a man to be square and honest in his dealings with an

outsider. In all my years and in all my trips over the southwest you are the first westerner to give me the double-cross.
You have that distinction.''

Then I turned my back upon him and walked to my tent.
His acquaintances left at once, and he quickly packed and
followed. Faithful old Doyle took up the duties of cook and
we gained, rather than missed by the change. Our supplies,
however, had been so depleted that we could not stay much
longer on the hunt.

By dint of much determination as to the manner and method
of my next hunt I managed to persuade myself that I could
make the best of this unlucky sojourn in the woods. No rifle,
no horse worth riding, no food to stay out our time—it was
indeed bad luck for me. After supper the tension relaxed.
Then I realized all the men were relieved. Only Romer regretted loss of Isbel. When the Doyles and Haughts saw how I
took my hard luck they seemed all the keener to make my
stay pleasant and profitable. Little they knew that their regard
was more to me than material benefits and comforts of the
trip. To travelers of the desert and hunters and riders of the
open there are always hard and uncomfortable and painful
situations to be met with. And in meeting these, if it can be
done with fortitude and spirit that win the respect of westerners, it is indeed a reward.

Next day, in defiance of a thing which never should be
considered—luck—I took Haught's rifle again, and my lazy,
sullen, intractable horse, and rode with Edd and George down
into Horton Thicket. At least I could not be cheated out of
fresh air and beautiful scenery.

We dismounted and tied our horses at the brook, and while
Edd took the hounds up into the dense thicket where the bears
made their beds, George and I followed a trail up the brook.
In exactly ten minutes the hounds gave tongue. They ran up
the thicket, which was favorable for us, and from their baying
I judged the bear trail to be warm. In the dense forest we
could not see five rods ahead. George averred that he did not
care to have a big cinnamon or a grizzly come running down
that black thicket. And as for myself I did not want one so
very exceedingly much. I tried to keep from letting the hounds

excite me, which effort utterly failed. We kept even with the
hounds until their baying fell off, and finally grew desultory,
and then ceased. "Guess they had the wrong end of his
trail," said George. With this exasperating feature of bear
and lion chases I was familiar. Most hounds, when they
struck a trail, could not tell in which direction the bear was
traveling. A really fine hound, however, like Buffalo Jones'
famous Don, or Scott Teague's Sampson or Haught's Old
Dan, would grow suspicious of a scent that gradually cooled,
and would eventually give it up. Young hounds would back-
track game as far as possible.

After waiting a while we returned to our horses, and presently Edd came back with the pack. "Big bear, but cold trail.
Called them off," was all he said. We mounted and rode
across the mouth of Horton Thicket round to the juniper
slopes, which I had occasion to remember. I even saw the
pine tree which I had so ignominiously climbed. How we
ridicule and scorn some of our perfectly natural actions—
afterwards! Edd had brought three of the pups that day,
two-year-olds as full of mischief as pups could be. They
jumped a bunch of deer and chased them out on the hard red
cedar covered ridges. We had a merry chase to head them off.
Edd gave them a tongue-lashing and thrashing at one and the
same time. I felt sorry for the pups. They had been so full of
frolic and fight. How crestfallen they appeared after Edd got
through! "Whaddaye mean," yelled Edd, in conclusion.
"Chasin' deer! . . . Do you think you're a lot of rabbit
dogs?" From the way the pups eyed Edd so sheepishly and
adoringly, I made certain they understood him perfectly, and
humbly confessed their error.

Old Tom and Old Dan had not come down off the slopes
with us after the pups. And upon our return both the old
hounds began to bay deep and fast. With shrill ki-yi the pups
bounded off, apparently frantic to make up for misbehavior.
Soon the whole pack was in full chorus. Edd and George
spurred into the brush, yelling encouragement to the hounds.
This day I managed to make my horse do a little of what I
wanted. To keep in sight of the Haught boys was indeed
beyond me; but I did not lose sound of them. This chase led

us up slope and down slope, through the brush and pine thickets, over bare ridges and into gullies; and eventually out into the basin, where the hounds got beyond hearing.

"One of them long, lean, hungry bears," remarked Edd. "He'd outrun any dogs."

Leisurely then we turned to the three-hour ride back to camp. Hot sun in the open, cool wind in the shade, dry smells of the forest, green and red and orange and purple of the foliage—these rendered the hours pleasant for me. When I reached camp I found Romer in trouble. He had cut his hand with a forbidden hunting knife. As he told me about it his face was a study and his explanation was astounding. When he finished I said: "You mean then that my hunting knife walked out of its sheath off my belt and followed you around and cut you of its own accord?"

"Aw, I—I—it—" he floundered.

Whereupon I lectured him about forbidden things and untruthfulness. His reply was: "But, Dad, it hurts like sixty. Won't you put somethin' on it?"

I dressed and bandaged the trifling cut for him, telling him the while how little Indian boys, when cut or kicked or bruised, never showed that they were hurt. "Huh!" he grunted. "Guess there's no Indian in me. . . . I must take after mother!"

That afternoon and night the hounds straggled in, Old Tom and Dan first, and then the others, one by one, fagged-out and foot-sore. Next morning, however, they appeared none the worse for their long chase. We went again to Horton Thicket to rout out a bear.

This time I remained on top of the rim with R. C. and Nielsen; and we took up a stand across the canyon, near where my first stand had been. Here we idled the hours away waiting for the hounds to start something. While walking along the rim I happened to look across the big cove that cut into the promontory, and way on the other slope what did I espy but a black bear. He appeared to be very small, or merely a cub. Running back to R. C. and Nielsen I told them, and we all took up our rifles. It occurred to me that the distance across this cove was too far for accurate shooting, but it never occurred to me to jump on my horse and ride around the head of the cove.

"He's not scared. Let's watch him," suggested R. C.

We saw this bear walk along, poke around, dig into the ground, go behind trees, come out again, and finally stand up on his hind feet and apparently reach for berries or something on a bush. R. C. bethought himself of his field-glass. After one look he exclaimed: "Say, fellows, he's a whopper of a bear! He'll weigh five hundred pounds. Just take a look at him!"

My turn with the glasses revealed to me that what I had imagined to be a cub was indeed a big bear. After Nielsen looked he said: "Never saw one so big in Norway."

"Well, look at that black scoundrel!" exclaimed R. C. "Standing up! Looking around! Wagging his head! . . . Say, you saw him first. Suppose you take some pegs at him."

"Wish Romer were here. I'd let him shoot at that bear," I replied. Then I got down on my knee, and aiming as closely as possible I fired. The report rang out in the stillness, making hollow echoes. We heard the bullet pat somewhere. So did the bear hear it. Curiously he looked around, as if something had struck near him. But scared he certainly was not. Then I shot four times in quick succession.

"Well, I'll be darned!" ejaculated R. C. "He heard the bullets hit and wonders what the dickens . . . Say, now he hears the reports! Look at him stand!"

"Boys, smoke him up," I said, after the manner of Haught's vernacular. So while I reloaded R. C. and Nielsen began to shoot. We had more fun out of it than the bear. Evidently he located us. Then he began to run, choosing the open slope by which he had come. I got five more shots at him as he crossed this space, and the last bullet puffed up dust under him, making him take a header down the slope into the thicket. Whereupon we all had a good laugh. Nielsen appeared particularly pleased over his first shots at a real live bear.

"Say, why didn't you think to ride round there?" queried R. C. thoughtfully. "He didn't see us. He wasn't scared. In a few minutes you could have been on the rim of that slope right over him. Got him sure!"

"R. C. why didn't you think to tell me to do that?" I retorted. "Why don't we ever think the right thing before it is too late?"

"That's our last chance this year—I feel it in my bones," declared R. C. mournfully.

His premonition turned out to be correct. Upon our arrival at camp we heard some very disquieting news. A neighbor of Haught's had taken the trouble to ride up to inform us about the epidemic of influenza. The strange disease was all over the country, in the cities, the villages, the cow-camps, the mines—everywhere. At first I thought Haught's informant was exaggerating a mere rumor. But when he told of the Indians dying on the reservations, and that in Flagstaff eighty people had succumbed in a few weeks—then I was thoroughly alarmed. Imperative was it indeed for me to make a decision at once. I made it instantly. We would break camp. So I told the men. Doyle was relieved and glad. He wanted to get home to his family. The Haughts, naturally, were sorry. My decision once arrived at, the next thing was to consider which way to travel. The long ten-day trip down into the basin, round by Payson, and up on the rim again, and so on to Flagstaff was not to be considered at all. The roads by way of Winslow and Holbrook were long and bad. Doyle wanted to attempt the old army road along the rim made by General Crook when he moved the captured Apaches to the reservation assigned to them. No travel over this road for many years! Haught looked dubious, but finally said we could chop our way through thickets, and haul the wagon empty up bad hills. The matter of decision was left to me. Decisions of such nature were not easy to make. The responsibility was great, but as the hunt had been for me it seemed incumbent upon me to accept responsibility. What made me hesitate at all was the fact that I had ridden five miles or more along the old Crook road. I remembered. I told Lee and I told Nielsen that we would find it tough going. Lee laughed like a cowboy: "We'll go a-hummin'," he said. Nielsen shrugged his brawny shoulders. What were obstacles to this man of the desert? I realized that his look had decided me.

"All right, men, we'll try the old Crook road," I said.

"Pack what you can up to the wagon to-day, and to-morrow early we'll break camp."

I walked with the Haughts from our camp across the brook to theirs, where we sat down in the warm sunshine. I made light of this hunting trip in which it had turned out I had no gun, no horse, no blankets, no rain-proof tent, no adequate amount of food supplies, and no good luck, except the wonderful good luck of being well, of seeing a magnificent country, of meeting some more fine westerners. But the Haughts appeared a little slow to grasp, or at least to credit my philosophy. We were just beginning to get acquainted. Their regret was that they had been unable to see me get a bear, a deer, a lion, and some turkeys. Their conviction, perhaps formed from association with many sportsman hunters, was that owing to my bad luck I could not and would not want to come again.

"See here, Haught," I said. "I've had a fine time. Now forget about this hunt. It's past. We'll plan another. Will you save next fall for me?"

"I shore will," he replied.

"Very well, then, it's settled. Say by August you and the boys cut a trail or two in and out of Horton Thicket. I'll send you money in advance to pay for this work, and get new hounds and outfit. I'll leave Flagstaff on September fifteenth. Meet you here September twenty-first, along about noon."

We shook hands upon the deal. It pleased me that the Haughts laughed at me yet appeared both surprised and happy. As I left I heard Edd remark: "Not a kick! . . . Meet him next year at noon! What do you know about thet?" This remark proved that he had paid me a compliment in eastern slang most likely assimilated from R. C. and Romer.

The rest of the afternoon our camp resembled a beehive, and next morning it was more like a bedlam. The horses were fresh, spirited, and they had tender backs; the burros stampeded because of some surreptitious trick of Romer's. But by noon we had all the outfit packed in the wagon. Considering the amount of stuff, and the long, rough climb up to the wagon, this was a most auspicious start. I hoped that it augured well for us, but while I hoped I had a gloomy foreboding. We bade good-bye to Haught and his son George. Edd offered to go with us as far as he knew the country, which distance was not many miles. So we set out upon our doubtful journey, our saddle-horses in front of the lumbering wagon.

We had five miles of fairly level road through open forest along the rim, and then we struck such a rocky jumble of downhill grade that the bundles fell off the wagon. They had to be tied on. When we came to a long slow slant uphill, a road of loose rocks, we made about one mile an hour. This slow travel worked havoc upon my mind. I wanted to hurry. I wanted to get out of the wilds. That awful rumor about influenza occupied my mind and struck cold fear into my heart. What of my family? No making the best of this! Slowly we toiled on. Sunset overtook us at a rocky ledge which had to be surmounted. With lassos on saddle horses in front of the two teams, all pulling hard, we overcame that obstacle. But at the next little hill, which we encountered about twilight, one of the team horses balked. Urging him, whipping him, served no purpose; and it had bad effect upon the other horses. Darkness was upon us with the camp-site Edd knew of still miles to the fore. No grass, no water for the horses! But we had to camp there. All hands set to work. It really was fun—it should have been fine for me—but my gloomy obsession to hurry obscured my mind. I marveled at old Doyle, over seventy, after that long, hard day, quickly and efficiently cooking a good hot supper. Romer had enjoyed the day. He said he was tired, but would like to stay up beside the mighty camp-fire Nielsen built. I had neither dark energy or spirit to oppose him. The night was dark and cold and windy; the fire felt so good that I almost went asleep beside it. We had no time to put up tents. I made our bed, crawled into it, stretched out with infinite relief; and the last thing I was aware of was Romer snuggling in beside me.

Morning brought an early bestirring of every one. We had to stir to get warm. The air nipped like cold pincers. All the horses were gone; we could not hear a bell. But Lee did not appear worried. I groaned in spirit. More delay! Gloom assailed me. Lee sallied out with his yellow dog Pups. I had forgotten the good quality of Pups, but not my dislike for him. He barked vociferously, and that annoyed me. R. C. and I helped Edd and Nielsen pack the wagon. We worked quick and hard. Then Doyle called us to breakfast. We had scarcely started to eat when we heard a jangle of bells and the pound of hoofs. I could not believe my ears. Our horses were lost. Nevertheless suddenly they appeared, driven by Lee riding bareback, and Pups barking his head off. We all jumped up with ropes and nose-bags to head off the horses, and soon had them secured. Not one missing! I asked Lee how in the world he had found that wild bunch in less than an hour. Lee laughed. "Pups. He rounded them up in no time."

Then I wanted to go away and hide behind a thicket and kick myself, but what I actually did was to give Pups part of my meat. I reproached myself for my injustice to him. How often had I been deceived in the surface appearance of people and things and dogs! Most of our judgments are wrong. We do not see clearly.

By nine o'clock we were meeting our first obstacle—the little hill at which the sorrel horse had balked. Lo! rested and full of grain, he balked again! He ruined our start. He spoiled the teams. Lee had more patience than I would have had. He unhitched the lead team and in place of the sorrel put a saddle horse called Pacer. Then Doyle tried again and surmounted the hill. Our saddle horses slowly worked ahead over as rocky and rough a road as I ever traveled. Most of the time we could see over the rim down into the basin. Along here the rim appeared to wave in gentle swells, heavily timbered and thickly rock-strewn, with heads of canyons opening down to our right. I saw deer tracks and turkey tracks, neither of which occasioned me any thrills now. About the middle of the afternoon Edd bade us farewell and turned back. We were sorry to see him go, but as all the country ahead of us was as unfamiliar to him as to us there seemed to be no urgent need of him.

We encountered a long, steep hill up which the teams, and our saddle horses combined, could not pull the wagon. We unpacked it, and each of us, Romer included, loaded a bundle or box in front of his saddle, and took it up the hill. Then the teams managed the wagon. This incident happened four times in less than as many miles. The team horses, having had a rest from hard labor, had softened, and this sudden return to strenuous pulling had made their shoulders sore. They either could not or would not pull. We covered less than ten miles that day, a very discouraging circumstance. We camped in a pine grove close to the rim, a splendid site that under favorable circumstances would have been enjoyable. At sunset R. C. and Nielsen and Romer saw a black bear down under the rim. The incident was so wonderful for Romer that it brightened my spirits. "A bear! A big bear, Dad! . . . I saw him! He was alive! He stood up—like this—wagging his head. Oh! I saw him!"

Our next day's progress was no less than a nightmare. Crawling along, unpacking and carrying, and packing again, we toiled up and down the interminable length of three almost impassable miles. When night overtook us it was in a bad place to camp. No grass, no water! A cold gale blew out of the west. It roared through the forest. It blew everything loose away in the darkness. It almost blew us away in our beds. The stars appeared radiantly coldly white up in the vast blue windy vault of the sky. A full moon soared majestically. Shadows crossed the weird moon-blanched forest glades.

At daylight we were all up, cramped, stiff, half frozen, mostly silent. The water left in the buckets was solid ice. Suddenly some one discovered that Nielsen was missing. The fact filled me with consternation and alarm. He might have walked in his sleep and fallen over the rim. What had become of him? All his outfit lay scattered round in his bed. In my bewilderment I imagined many things, even to the extreme that he might have left us in the lurch. But when I got to that sad pass of mind I suddenly awakened as if out of an evil dream. My worry, my hurry had obsessed me. High time indeed was it for me to meet this situation as I had met other difficult ones. To this end I went out away from camp, and forgot myself, my imagined possibilities, and thought of my present responsibility, and the issue at hand. That instant I realized my injustice toward Nielsen, and reproached myself. Upon my return to camp Nielsen was there, warming one hand over the camp-fire and holding a cup of coffee in the other.

"Nielsen, you gave us a scare. Please explain," I said.

"Yes, sir. Last night I was worried. I couldn't sleep. I got to thinking we were practically lost. Some one ought to find out what was ahead of us. So I got up and followed the road. Bright moonlight. I walked all the rest of the night. And that's all, sir."

I liked Nielsen's looks then. He reminded me of Jim Emett, the Mormon giant to whom difficulties and obstacles were but spurs to achievement. Such men could not be defeated.

"Well, what did you find out?" I inquired.

"Change of conditions, sir," he replied, as a mate to his captain. "Only one more steep hill so far as I went. But we'll have to cut through thickets and logs. From here on the road is all grown over. About ten miles west we turn off the rim down a ridge."

That about the turning-off place was indeed good news. I thanked Nielsen. And Doyle appeared immensely relieved. The packing and carrying had begun to tell on us. Pups ingratiated himself into my affections. He found out that he could coax meat and biscuit from me. We had three axes and a hatchet; and these we did not pack in the wagon. When Doyle finally got the teams started Lee and Nielsen and R. C. and I went ahead to clear the road. Soon we were halted by thickets of pines, some of which were six inches in diameter at the base. The road had ceased to be rocky, and that, no doubt, was the reason pine thickets had grown up on it. The wagon kept right at our heels, and many times had to wait. We cut a way through thickets, tore rotten logs to pieces, threw stumps aside, and moved windfalls. Brawny Nielsen seemed ten men in one! What a swath he hacked with his big axe! When I rested, which circumstance grew oftener and oftener, I had to watch Nielsen with his magnificent swing of the axe, or with his mighty heave on a log. Time and again he lifted tree trunks out of the road. He sweat till he was wringing wet. Neither that day nor the next would we have ever gotten far along that stretch of thicketed and obstructed road had it not been for Nielsen.

At sunset we found ourselves at the summit of a long slowly ascending hill, deeply forested. It took all the horses together to pull the wagon to the top. Thus when we started down a steep curve, horses and men both were tired. I was ahead riding beside Romer. Nielsen and R. C. were next, and Lee had fallen in behind the wagon. As I turned the sharp curve I saw not fifty feet below me a huge log obstructing the road.

"Look out! Stop!" I yelled, looking back.

But I was too late. The horses could not hold back the heavily laden wagon, and they broke into a gallop. I saw Doyle's face turn white—heard him yell. Then I spurred my horse to the side. Romer was slow or frightened. I screamed at him to get off the road. My heart sank sick within me! Surely he would be run down. As his pony Rye jumped out of the way the shoulder of the black horse, on the off side, struck him a glancing blow. Then the big team hurdled the log, the tongue struck with a crash, the wagon stopped with a lurch, and Doyle was thrown from his seat.

Quick as a flash Nielsen was on the spot beside the team. The bay horse was down. The black horse was trying to break away. Nielsen cut and pulled the bay free of the harness, and Lee came tearing down to grasp and hold the black.

Like a fool I ran around trying to help somehow, but I did not know what to do. I smelled and then saw blood, which fact convinced me of disaster. Only the black horse that had hurdled the log made any effort to tear away. The other lay quiet. When finally it was extricated we found that the horse had a bad cut in the breast made by a snag on the log. We could find no damage done to the wagon. The harness Nielsen had cut could be mended quickly. What a fortunate outcome to what had seemed a very grave accident! I was thankful indeed. But not soon would I forget the sight of Romer in front of that plunging wagon.

With the horses and a rope we hauled the log to one side of the road, and hitching up again we proceeded on our way. Once I dropped back and asked Doyle if he was all right. "Fine as a fiddle," he shouted. "This's play to what we teamsters had in the early days." And verily somehow I could see the truth of that. A mile farther on we made camp; and all of us were hungry, weary, and quiet.

Doyle proved a remarkable example to us younger men. Next morning he crawled out before any one else, and his call was cheery. I was scarcely able to get out of my bed, but I was ashamed to lie there an instant after I heard Doyle. Possibly my eyesight was dulled by exhaustion when it caused me to see myself as a worn, unshaven, wrinkled wretch. Romer-boy did not hop out with his usual alacrity. R. C. had to roll over in his bed and get up on all fours.

We had scant rations for three more days. It behooved us to work and waste not an hour. All morning, at the pace of a snail it seemed, we chopped and lifted and hauled our way along that old Crook road. Not since my trip down the Santa Rosa river in Mexico had I labored so strenuously.

At noon we came to the turning-off junction, an old blazed road Doyle had some vague knowledge of. "It must lead to Jones' ranch," Doyle kept saying. "Anyway, we've got to take it." North was our direction. And to our surprise, and exceeding gladness, the road down this ridge proved to be a highway compared to what we had passed. In the open forest we had to follow it altogether by the blazes on the trees. But with all our eyes alert that was easy. The grade was down hill, so that we traveled fast, covering four miles an hour. Occasionally a log or thicket halted rapid progress. Toward the end of the afternoon sheep and cattle trails joined the now well-defined road, and we knew we were approaching a ranch. I walked, or rather limped the last mile, for the very good reason that I could not longer bear the trot of my horse. The forest grew more open, with smaller pines, and fewer thickets. At sunset I came out upon the brow of a deep barren-looking canyon, in the middle of which squatted some old ruined log-cabins. Deserted! Alas for my visions of a cup of cold milk. For hours they had haunted me. When Doyle saw the broken-down cabins and corrals he yelled: "Boys, it's Jones' Ranch. I've been here. We're only three miles from Long Valley and the main road!"

Elated we certainly were. And we rushed down the steep hill to look for water. All our drinking water was gone, and the horses had not slaked their thirst for two days. Separating we rode up and down the canyon. R. C. and Romer found running water. Thereupon with immense relief and joy we pitched camp near the cabins, forgetting our aches and pains in the certainty of deliverance.

What a cold, dismal, bleak, stony, and lonesome place! We unpacked only bedding, and our little store of food. And huddled around the camp-fire we waited upon Doyle's cooking. The old pioneer talked while he worked.

"Jones' ranch!—I knew Jones in the early days. And I've heard of him lately. Thirty years ago he rode a prairie schooner down into this canyon. He had his wife, a fine, strong girl, and he had a gun, an axe, some chuck, a few horses and cattle, and not much else. He built him that cabin there and began the real old pioneering of the early days. He raised cattle. He freighted to the settlements twice a year. In twenty-five years he had three strapping boys and a girl just as strapping. And he had a fortune in cattle. Then he sold his stock and left this ranch. He wanted to give his faithful wife and his children some of the comforts and luxuries and advantages of civilization. The war came. His sons did not wait for the draft. They entered the army. I heard a story about Abe Jones, the old man's first boy. Abe was a quiet sort of chap. When he got to the army training camp a sergeant asked Abe if he could shoot. Abe said: 'Nope, not much.' So they gave him a rifle and told him to shoot at the near target. Abe looked at it sort of funny like and he picked out the farthest target at one thousand yards. And he hit the bull's eye ten times straight running. 'Hey!' gasped the sergeant, 'you long, lanky galoot! You said you couldn't shoot.' Abe sort of laughed. 'Reckon I was thinkin' about what Dad called shootin'.' . . . Well, Abe and his brothers got to France to the front. Abe was a sharpshooter. He was killed at Argonne. Both his brothers were wounded. They're over there yet . . . I met a man not long ago who'd seen Jones recently. And the old pioneer said he and his wife would like to be back home. And home to them means right here—Jones' Ranch!"

Doyle's story affected me profoundly. What a theme for a novel! I walked away from the camp-fire into the dark, lonely, melancholy Arizona night. The ruined cabins, the broken-down corrals, the stone fence, the wash where water ran at wet season—all had subtly changed for me. Leaning in the doorway of the one-room cabin that had been home for these Joneses I was stirred to my depths. Their spirits abided in that lonely hut. At least I felt something there—something strange, great, simple, inevitable, tragic as life itself. Yet what could have been more beautiful, more splendid than the life of Jones, and his wife, and daughter, and sons, especially Abe? Abe Jones! The name haunted me. In one clear divining flash I saw the life of the lad. I yearned with tremendous passion for the power to tell the simplicity, the ruggedness, the pathos and the glory of his story. The moan of wind in the pines seemed a requiem for the boy who had prattled and romped and played under them, who had chopped and shot and rode under them. Into his manhood had gone something of their strength and nature.

We sought our beds early. The night down in that deep, open canyon was the coldest we had experienced. I slept but little. At dawn all was hoar-white with frost. It crackled under foot. The air had a stinging bite. Yet how sweet, pure, cold to breathe!

Doyle's cheery: "Come and get it," was welcome call to breakfast. Lee and Pups drove the horses into one of the old corrals. In an hour, while the frost was yet hard and white, we were ready to start. Then Doyle somewhat chilled our hopes: "Twenty years ago there was a bad road out of here. Maybe one's been made since."

But one had not been made. And the old road had not been used for years. Right at the outset we struck a long, steep, winding, rocky road. We got stalled at the very foot of it. More toil! Unloading the wagon we packed on our saddles the whole load more than a mile up this last and crowning obstacle. Then it took all the horses together to pull the empty wagon up to a level. By that time sunset had overtaken us. Where had the hours gone? Nine hours to go one mile! But there had to be an end to our agonies. By twilight we trotted down into Long Valley, and crossed the main road to camp in a grove we remembered well. We partook of a meagre supper, but we were happy. And bed that night on a thick layer of soft pine needles, in a spot protected from the cold wind, was immensely comfortable.

Lee woke the crowd next morning. "All rustle," he yelled. "Thirty-five miles to Mormon Lake. Good road. We'll camp there to-night."

How strange that the eagerness to get home now could only be compared to the wild desire for the woods a few weeks back! We made an early start. The team horses knew that road. They knew they were now on the way home. What difference that made! Jaded as they were they trotted along with a briskness never seen before on that trip. It began to be a job for us to keep up with Lee, who was on the wagon. Unless a rider is accustomed to horseback almost all of the time a continuous trot on a hard road will soon stove him up. My horse had an atrocious trot. Time and again I had to fall behind to a walk and then lope ahead to catch up. I welcomed the hills that necessitated Lee walking the teams.

At noon we halted in a grassy grove for an hour's rest. That seemed a precious hour, but to start again was painful. I noticed that Romer-boy no longer rode out far in front, nor did he chase squirrels with Pups. He sagged, twisted and turned, and lolled in his saddle. Thereafter I tried to keep close to him. But that was not easy, for he suspected me of seeing how tired he was, and kept away from me. Thereafter I took to spying upon him from some distance behind. We trotted and walked, trotted and walked the long miles. Arizona miles were twice as long as ordinary properly measured miles. An event of the afternoon was to meet some Mexican sheepherders, driving a flock south. Nielsen got some fresh mutton from them. Toward sunset I caught Romer hanging over his saddle. Then I rode up to him. "Son, are you tired?" I asked. "Oh, Dad, I sure am, but I'm going to ride Rye to Mormon Lake." I believed he would accomplish it. His saddle slipped, letting him down. I saw him fall. When he made no effort to get up I was frightened. Rye stood perfectly still over him. I leaped off and ran to the lad. He had hit his head on a stone, drawing the blood, and appeared to be stunned. I lifted him, holding him up, while somebody got some water. We bathed his face and washed off the blood. Presently he revived, and smiled at me, and staggered out of my hold.

"Helluva note that saddle slipped!" he complained. Manifestly he had acquired some of Joe Isbel's strong language. Possibly he might have acquired some other of the cowboy's traits, for he asked to have his saddle straightened and to be put on his horse. I had misgivings, but I could not resist him then. I lifted him upon Rye. Once more our cavalcade got under way.

Sunset, twilight, night came as we trotted on and on. We faced a cold wind. The forest was black, gloomy, full of shadows. Lee gave us all we could do to keep up with him. At eight o'clock, two hours after dark, we reached the southern end of Mormon Lake. A gale, cold as ice, blew off the water from the north. Half a dozen huge pine trees stood on the only level ground near at hand. "Nielsen, fire—pronto!" I yelled. "Aye, sir," he shouted, in his deep voice. Then what with hurry and bustle to get my bedding and packs, and to thresh my tingling fingers, and press my frozen ears, I was selfishly busy a few minutes before I thought of Romer.

Nielsen had started a fire, that blazed and roared with burning pine needles. The blaze blew low, almost on a level with the ground, and a stream of red sparks flew off into the woods. I was afraid of forest fire. But what a welcome sight that golden flame! It lighted up a wide space, showing the huge pines, gloom-encircled, and a pale glimmer of the lake beyond. The fragrance of burning pine greeted my nostrils.

Dragging my bags I hurried toward the fire. Nielsen was building a barricade of rocks to block the flying sparks. Suddenly I espied Romer. He sat on a log close to the blaze. His position struck me as singular, so I dropped my burdens and went to him. He had on a heavy coat over sweater and under coat, which made him resemble a little old man. His sombrero was slouched down sidewise, his gloved hands were folded across his knees, his body sagged a little to one side, his head drooped. He was asleep. I got around so I could see his face in the firelight. Pale, weary, a little sad, very youthful and yet determined! A bloody bruise showed over his temple. He had said he would ride all the way to Mormon Lake and he had done it. Never, never will that picture fade from my memory! Dear, brave, wild, little lad! He had made for me a magnificent success of this fruitless hunting trip. I hoped and prayed then that when he grew to man's estate, and faced the long rides down the hard roads of life, he would meet them and achieve them as he had the weary thirty-five Arizona miles from Long Valley to Mormon Lake.

Mutton tasted good that night around our camp-fire; and Romer ate a generous portion. A ranger from the station near there visited us, and two young ranchers, who told us that the influenza epidemic was waning. This was news to be thankful for. Moreover, I hired the two ranchers to hurry us by auto to Flagstaff on the morrow. So right there at Mormon Lake ended our privations.

Under one of the huge pines I scraped up a pile of needles, made Romer's bed in it, heated a blanket and wrapped him in it. Almost he was asleep when he said: "Some ride, Dad—Good-night."

Later, beside him, I lay awake a while, watching the sparks fly, and the shadows flit, feeling the cold wind on my face, listening to the crackle of the fire and the roar of the gale.

IV

Eventually R. C. and Romer and I arrived in Los Angeles to find all well with our people, which fact was indeed something to rejoice over. Hardly had this 1918 trip ended before I began to plan for that of 1919. But I did not realize how much in earnest I was until I received word that both Lee Doyle in Flagstaff and Nielsen in San Pedro were very ill with influenza. Lee all but died, and Nielsen, afterward, told me he would rather die than have the "flu" again. To my great relief, however, they recovered.

From that time then it pleased me to begin to plan for my 1919 hunting trip. I can never do anything reasonably. I always overdo everything. But what happiness I derive from anticipation! When I am not working I live in dreams, partly of the past, but mostly of the future. A man should live only in the present.

I gave Lee instructions to go about in his own way buying teams, saddle horses, and wagons. For Christmas I sent him a .35 Remington rifle. Mr. Haught got instructions to add some new dogs to his pack. I sent Edd also a .35 Remington, and made Nielsen presents of two guns. In January Nielsen and I went to Picacho, on the lower Colorado river, and then north to Death Valley. So that I kept in touch with these men and did not allow their enthusiasm to wane. For myself and R. C. I had the fun of ordering tents and woolen blankets, and everything that we did not have on our 1918 trip. But owing to the war it was difficult to obtain goods of any description. To make sure of getting a .30 Gov't Winchester I ordered from four different firms, including the Winchester Co. None of them had such a rifle in stock, but all would try to find one. The upshot of this deal was that, when after months I despaired of getting any, they all sent me a rifle at the same time. So I found myself with four, all the same caliber of course, but of different style and finish. When I saw them and thought of the Haughts I had to laugh. One was beautifully engraved, and inlaid with gold—the most elaborate .30 Gov't the Winchester people had ever built. Another was a walnut-stocked, shot-gun butted, fancy checkered take-down. This one I presented to R. C. The third was a plain ordinary rifle with solid frame. And the last was a carbine model, which I gave to Nielsen.

During the summer at Avalon I used to take the solid frame rifle, and climb the hills to practice on targets. At Clemente Island I used to shoot at the ravens. I had a grudge against ravens there for picking the eyes out of newly born lambs. At five hundred yards a raven was in danger from me. I could make one jump at even a thousand yards. These .30 Gov't 1906 rifles with 150-grain bullet are the most wonderful shooting arms I ever tried. I became expert at inanimate targets.

From time to time I heard encouraging news from Lee about horses. Edd wrote me about lion tracks in the snow, and lynx up cedar trees, and gobblers four feet high, and that there was sure to be a good crop of acorns, and therefore some bears. He told me about a big grizzly cow-killer being chased and shot in Chevelon Canyon. News about hounds, however, was slow in coming. Dogs were difficult to find. At length Haught wrote me that he had secured two; and in this same letter he said the boys were cutting trails down under the rim.

Everything pertaining to my cherished plans appeared to be turning out well. But during this time I spent five months at hard work and intense emotional strain, writing the longest novel I ever attempted; and I overtaxed my endurance. By the middle of June, when I finished, I was tired out. That would not have mattered if I had not hurt my back in an eleven-hour fight with a giant broadbill swordfish. This strain kept me from getting in my usual physical trim. I could not climb the hills, or exert myself. Swimming hurt me more than anything. So I had to be careful and wait until my back slowly got better. By September it had improved, but not enough to make me feel any thrills over horseback riding. It seemed to me that I would be compelled to go ahead and actually work the pain out of my back, an ordeal through which I had passed before, and surely dreaded.

During the summer I had purchased a famous chestnut sorrel horse named Don Carlos. He was much in demand among the motion-picture companies doing western plays; and was really too fine and splendid a horse to be put to the risks common to the movies. I saw him first at Palm Springs, down in southern California, where my book *Desert Gold* was being made into a motion-picture. Don would not have failed to strike any one as being a wonderful horse. He was tremendously high and rangy and powerful in build, yet graceful withal, a sleek, shiny chestnut red in color, with fine legs, broad chest, and a magnificent head. I rode him only once before I bought him, and that was before I hurt my back. His stride was what one would expect from sight of him; his trot seemed to tear me to pieces; his spirit was such that he wanted to prance all the time. But in spite of his spirit he was a pet. And how he could run! Nielsen took Don to Flagstaff by express. And when Nielsen wrote me he said all of Flagstaff came down to the station to see the famous Don

Carlos. The car in which he had traveled was backed along-side a platform. Don refused to step on the boards they placed from platform to car. He did not trust them. Don's intelligence had been sharpened by his experience with the movies. Nielsen tried to lead, to coax, and to drive Don to step on the board walk. Don would not go. But suddenly he snorted, and jumped the space clear, to plunge and pound down upon the platform, scattering the crowd like quail.

The day before my departure from Los Angeles was almost as terrible an ordeal as I anticipated would be my first day's ride on Don Carlos. And this ordeal consisted of listening to Romer's passionate appeals and importunities to let him go on the hunt. My only defence was that he must not be taken from school. School forsooth! He was way ahead of his class. If he got behind he could make it up. I talked and argued. Once he lost his temper, a rare thing with him, and said he would run away from school, ride on a freight train to Flagstaff, steal a horse and track me to my camp. I could not say very much in reply to this threat, because I remembered that I had made worse to my father, and carried it out. I had to talk sense to Romer. Often we had spoken of a wonderful hunt in Africa some day, when he was old enough; and I happened upon a good argument. I said: "You'll miss a year out of school then. It won't be so very long. Don't you think you ought to stay in school faithfully now?" So in the end I got away from him, victorious, though not wholly happy. The truth was I wanted him to go.

My Jap cook Takahashi met me in Flagstaff. He was a very short, very broad, very muscular little fellow with a brown, strong face, more pleasant than usually seen in Orientals. Secretly I had made sure that in Takahashi I had discovered a treasure, but I was careful to conceal this conviction from R. C., the Doyles, and Nielsen. They were glad to see him with us, but they manifestly did not, expect wonders.

How brief the span of a year! Here I was in Flagstaff again outfitting for another hunt. It seemed incredible. It revived that old haunting thought about the shortness of life. But in spite of that or perhaps more because of it the pleasure was all the keener. In truth the only drawback to this start was the absence of Romer, and my poor physical condition. R. C. appeared to be in fine fettle.

But I was not well. In the mornings I could scarcely arise, and when I did so I could hardly straighten myself. More than once I grew doubtful of my strength to undertake such a hard trip. This doubt I fought fiercely, for I knew that the right thing for me to do was to go—to stand the pain and hardship—to toil along until my old strength and elasticity returned. What an opportunity to try out my favorite theory! For I believed that labor and pain were good for mankind—that strenuous life in the open would cure any bodily ill.

On September fourteenth Edd and George drifted into Flagstaff to join us, and their report of game and water and grass and acorns was so favorable that I would have gone if I had been unable to ride on anything but a wagon. We got away on September fifteenth at two-thirty o'clock with such an outfit as I had never had in all my many trips put together. We had a string of saddle horses besides those the men rode. They were surely a spirited bunch; and that first day it was indeed a job to keep them with us. Out of sheer defiance with myself I started on Don Carlos. He was no trouble, except that it took all my strength to hold him in. He tossed his head, champed his bit, and pranced sideways along the streets of Flagstaff, manifestly to show off his brand new black Mexican saddle, with silver trappings and tapaderos. I was sure that he did not do that to show me off. But Don liked to dance and prance along before a crowd, a habit that he had acquired with the motion pictures.

Lee and Nielsen and George had their difficulties driving the free horses. Takahashi rode a little buckskin Navajo mustang. An evidence of how extremely short the Jap's legs were made itself plain in the fact that stirrups could not be fixed so he could reach them with his feet. When he used any support at all he stuck his feet through the straps above the stirrups. How funny his squat, broad figure looked in a saddle! Evidently he was not accustomed to horses. When I saw the mustang roll the white of his eyes and glance back at Takahashi then I knew something would happen sooner or later.

Nineteen miles on Don Carlos reduced me to a miserable

aching specimen of manhood. But what made me endure and go on and finish to camp was the strange fact that the longer I rode the less my back pained. Other parts of my anatomy, however, grew sorer as we progressed. Don Carlos pleased me immensely, only I feared he was too much horse for me. A Mormon friend of mine, an Indian trader, looked Don over in Flagstaff, and pronounced him: "Shore one grand hoss!" This man had broken many wild horses, and his compliment pleased me. All the same the nineteen miles on Don hurt my vanity almost as much as my body.

We camped in a cedar pasture off the main road. This road was a new one for us to take to our hunting grounds. I was too bunged up to help Nielsen pitch our tent. In fact when I sat down I was anchored. Still I could use my eyes, and that made life worth living. Sunset was a gorgeous spectacle. The San Francisco Peaks were shrouded in purple storm-clouds, and the west was all gold and silver, with low clouds rimmed in red. This sunset ended in a great flare of dull magenta with a background of purple.

That evening was the try-out of our new chuck-box and chef. I had supplied the men with their own outfit and supplies, to do with as they liked, an arrangement I found to be most satisfactory. Takahashi was to take care of R. C. and me. In less than half an hour from the time the Jap lighted a fire he served the best supper I ever had in camp anywhere. R. C. lauded him to the skies. And I began to think I could unburden myself of my conviction.

I did not awaken to the old zest and thrill of the open. Something was wrong with me. The sunset, the campfire, the dark clear night with its trains of stars, the distant yelp of coyotes—these seemed less to me than what I had hoped for. My feelings were locked round my discomfort and pain.

About noon next day we rode out of the cedars into the open desert—a rolling, level land covered with fine grass, and yellow daisies, Indian paint brush, and a golden flowering weed. This luxuriance attested to the copious and recent rains. They had been a boon to dry Arizona. No sage showed or greasewood, and very few rocks. The sun burned hot. I gazed out at the desert, and the cloud pageant in the sky, trying hard to forget myself, and to see what I knew was there for me. Rolling columnar white and cream clouds, majestic and beautiful, formed storms off on the horizon. Sunset on the open desert that afternoon was singularly characteristic of Arizona—purple and gold and red, with long lanes of blue between the colored cloud banks.

We made camp at Meteor Crater, one of the many wonders of this wonderland. It was a huge hole in the earth over five hundred feet deep, said to have been made by a meteor burying itself there. Seen from the outside the slope was gradual up to the edges, which were scalloped and irregular; on the inside the walls were precipitous. Our camp was on the windy desert, a long sweeping range of grass, sloping down, dotted with cattle, with buttes and mountains in the distance. Most of my sensations of the day partook of the nature of woe.

September seventeenth bade fair to be my worst day—at least I did not see how any other could ever be so bad. Glaring hot sun—reflected heat from the bare road—dust and sand and wind! Particularly hard on me were what the Arizonians called dust-devils, whirlwinds of sand. On and off I walked a good many miles, the latter of which I hobbled. Don Carlos did not know what to make of this. He eyed me, and nosed me, and tossed his head as if to say I was a strange rider for him. Like my mustang, Night, he would not stand to be mounted. When I touched the stirrup that was a signal to go. He had been trained to it. As he was nearly seventeen hands high, and as I could not get my foot in the stirrup from level ground, to mount him in my condition seemed little less than terrible. I always held back out of sight when I attempted this. Many times I failed. Once I fell flat and lay a moment in the dust. Don Carlos looked down upon me in a way I imagined was sympathetic. At least he bent his noble head and smelled at me. I scrambled to my feet, led him round into a low place, and drawing a deep breath, and nerving myself to endure the pain like a stab, I got into the saddle again.

Two things sustained me in this ordeal, which was the cruelest horseback ride I ever had—first, the conviction that I could cure my ills by enduring the agony of violent action, of hot sun, of hard bed; and secondly, the knowledge that after it was all over the remembrance of hardship and achievement would be singularly sweet. So it had been in the case of the five days on the old Crook road in 1918, when extreme worry and tremendous exertion had made the hours hideous. So it had been with other arduous and poignant experiences. A poet said that the crown of sorrow was in remembering happier times: I believed that there was a great deal of happiness in remembering times of stress, of despair, of extreme and hazardous effort. Anyway, without these two feelings in my mind I would have given up riding Don Carlos that day, and have abandoned the trip.

We covered twenty-two miles by sundown, a rather poor day's showing; and camped on the bare flat desert, using water and wood we had packed with us. The last thing I remembered, as my eyes closed heavily, was what a blessing it was to rest and to sleep.

Next day we sheered off to the southward, heading toward Chevelon Butte, a black cedared mountain, rising lone out of the desert, thirty miles away. We crossed two streams bank full of water, a circumstance I never before saw in Arizona. Everywhere too the grass was high. We climbed gradually all day, everybody sunburned and weary, the horses settling down to save themselves; and we camped high up on the desert plateau, six thousand feet above sea level, where it was windy, cool, and fragrant with sage and cedar. Except the first few, the hours of this day each marked a little less torture for me; but at that I fell off Don Carlos when we halted. And I was not able to do my share of the camp work. R. C. was not as spry and chipper as I had seen him, a fact from which I gathered infinite consolation. Misery loves company.

A storm threatened. All the west was purple under on-coming purple clouds. At sight of this something strange and subtle, yet familiar, revived in me. It made me feel a little more like the self I thought I knew. So I watched the lightning flare and string along the horizon. Some time in the night thunder awakened me. The imminence of a severe storm forced us to roll out and look after the tent. What a pitch black night! Down through the murky, weird blackness shot a wonderful zigzag rope of lightning, blue-white, dazzling; and it disintegrated, leaving segments of fire in the air. All this showed in a swift flash—then we were absolutely blind. I could not see for several moments. It rained a little. Only the edge of the storm touched us. Thunder rolled and boomed along the battlements, deep and rumbling and detonating.

No dust or heat next morning! The desert floor appeared clean and damp, with fresh gray sage and shining bunches of cedar. We climbed into the high cedars, and then to the piñons, and then to the junipers and pines. Climbing so out of desert to forestland was a gradual and accumulating joy to me. What contrast in vegetation, in air, in color! Still the forest consisted of small trees. Not until next day did we climb farther to the deepening, darkening forest, and at last to the silver spruce. That camp, the fifth night out, was beside a lake of surface water, where we had our first big camp-fire.

September twenty-first and ten miles from Beaver Dam Canyon, where a year before I had planned to meet Haught this day and date at noon! I could make that appointment, saddle-sore and weary as I was, but I doubted we could get the wagons there. The forest ground was soft. All the little swales were full of water. How pleasant, how welcome, how beautiful and lonely the wild forestland! We made advance slowly. It was afternoon by the time we reached the rim road, and four o'clock when we halted at the exact spot where we had left our wagon the year before.

Lee determined to drive the wagons down over the rocky benches into Beaver Dam Canyon; and to that end he and the men began to cut pines, drag logs, and roll stones.

R. C. and I rode down through the forest, crossing half a dozen swift little streams of amber water, where a year before all had been dry as tinder. We found Haught's camp in a grove of yellowing aspens. Haught was there to meet us. He had not changed any more than the rugged pine tree under which a year past we had made our agreement. He wore the same blue shirt and the old black sombrero.

"Hello Haught," was my greeting, as I dismounted and pulled out my watch. "I'm four hours and a quarter late.

Sorry. I could have made it, but didn't want to leave the wagons.''

"Wal, wal, I shore am glad to see you," he replied, with a keen flash in his hazel eyes and a smile on his craggy face. "I reckoned you'd make it. How are you? Look sort of fagged.''

"Just about all in, Haught," I replied, as we shook hands.

Then Copple appeared, swaggering out of the aspens. He was the man I met in Payson and who so kindly had made me take his rifle. I had engaged him also for this hunt. A brawny man he was, with powerful shoulders, swarthy-skinned, and dark-eyed, looking indeed the Indian blood he claimed.

"Wouldn't have recognized you anywhere's else," he said.

These keen-eyed outdoor men at a glance saw the havoc work and pain had played with me. They were solicitous, and when I explained my condition they made light of that, and showed relief that I was not ill. "Saw wood an' rustle around," said Haught. And Copple said: "He needs venison an' bear meat.''

They rode back with us up to the wagons. Copple had been a freighter. He picked out a way to drive down into the canyon. So rough and steep it was that I did not believe driving down would be possible. But with axes and pick and shovel, and a heaving of rocks, they worked a road that Lee drove down. Some places were almost straight down. But the ground was soft, hoofs and wheels sank deeply, and though one wagon lurched almost over, and the heavily laden chuck-wagon almost hurdled the team, Lee made the bad places without accident. Two hours after our arrival, such was the labor of many strong hands, we reached our old camp ground. One thing was certain, however, and that was we would never get back up the way we came down.

Except for a luxuriance of grass and ferns, and two babbling streams of water, our old camp ground had not changed. I sat down with mingled emotions. How familiarly beautiful and lonely this canyon glade! The great pines and spruces looked down upon me with a benediction. How serene, passionless, strong they seemed! It was only men who changed in brief time. The long year of worry and dread and toil and pain had passed. It was nothing. On the soft, fragrant, pine-scented breeze came a whispering of welcome from the forestland: "You are here again. Live now—in the present."

Takahashi beamed upon me: "More better place to camp," he said, grinning. Already the Jap had won my admiration and liking. His ability excited my interest, and I wanted to know more about him. As to this camp-site being a joy compared to the ones stretched back along the road he was assuredly right. That night we did no more than eat and unroll our beds. But next day there set in the pleasant tasks of unpacking, putting up tents and flies, cutting spruce for thick, soft beds, and a hundred odd jobs dear to every camper. Takahashi would not have any one help him. He dug a wide space for fires, erected a stone windbreak, and made two ovens out of baked mud, the like of which, and the cleverness of which I had never seen. He was a whirlwind for work.

The matter of firewood always concerned Nielsen and me more than any one. Nielsen was a Norwegian, raised as a boy to use a crosscut saw; and as for me I was a connoisseur in camp-fires and a lover of them. Hence we had brought a crosscut saw—a long one with two handles. I remembered from the former year a huge dead pine that had towered bleached and white at the edge of the glade. It stood there still. The storms and blasts of another winter had not changed it in the least. It was five feet thick at the base and solid. Nielsen chopped a notch in it on the lower side, and then he and Edd began to saw into it on the other. I saw the first tremor of the lofty top. Then soon it shivered all the way down, gave forth a loud crack, swayed slowly, and fell majestically, to strike with a thundering crash. Only the top of this pine broke in the fall, but there were splinters and knots and branches enough to fill a wagon. These we carried up to our camp-fire.

Then the boys sawed off half a dozen four-foot sections, which served as fine, solid, flat tables for comfort around camp. The method of using a crosscut saw was for two men to take a stand opposite one another, with the log between. The handles of the saw stood upright. Each man should pull easily and steadily toward himself, but should not push back nor bear down. It looked a rhythmic, manly exercise, and not arduous. But what an illusion! Nielsen and Copple were the only ones that day who could saw wholly through the thick log without resting. Later Takahashi turned out to be as good, if not better, than either of them, but we had that, as well as many other wonderful facts, to learn about the Jap.

"Come on," said R. C. to me, invitingly. "You've been talking about this crosscut saw game. I'll bet you find it harder than pulling on a swordfish."

Pride goes before a fall! I knew that in my condition I could do little with the saw, but I had to try. R. C. was still fresh when I had to rest. Perhaps no one except myself realized the weakness of my back, but the truth was a couple of dozen pulls on that saw almost made me collapse. Wherefore I grew furious with myself and swore I would do it or die. I sawed till I fell over—then I rested and went back at it. Half an hour of this kind of exercise gave me a stab in my left side infinitely sharper than the pain in my back. Also it made me wringing wet, hot as fire, and as breathless as if I had run a mile up hill. That experience determined me to stick to crosscut sawing every day. Next morning I approached it with enthusiasm, yet with misgivings. I could not keep my breath. Pain I could and did bear without letting on. But to have to stop was humiliating. If I tried to keep up with the sturdy Haught boys, or with the brawny Copple or the giant Nielsen, soon I would be compelled to keel over. In the sawing through a four-foot section of log I had to rest eight times. They all had a great deal of fun out of it, and I pretended to be good natured, but to me who had always been so vigorous and active and enduring it was not fun. It was tragic. But all was not gloom for me. This very afternoon Nielsen, the giant, showed that a stiff climb out of the canyon, at that eight thousand feet altitude, completely floored him. Yet I accomplished that with comparative ease. I could climb, which seemed proof that I was gaining. A man becomes used to certain labors and exercises. I thought the crosscut saw a wonderful tool to train a man, but it must require time. It harked back to pioneer days when men were men. Nielsen said he had lived among Mexican boys who sawed logs for nineteen cents apiece and earned seven dollars a day. Copple said three minutes was good time to saw a four-foot log in two pieces. So much for physical condition! As for firewood, for which our crosscut saw was intended, pitch pine and yellow pine and spruce were all odorous and inflammable woods, but they did not make good firewood. Dead aspen was good; dead oak the best. It burned to red hot coals with little smoke. As for camp-fires, any kind of dry wood pleased, smoke or no smoke. In fact I loved the smell and color of woodsmoke, in spite of the fact that it made my eyes smart.

By October first, which was the opening day of the hunting season, I had labored at various exercises until I felt fit to pack a rifle through the woods. R. C. and I went out alone on foot. Not by any means was the day auspicious. The sun tried to show through a steely haze, making only a pale shift of sunshine. And the air was rather chilly. Enthusiasm, however, knew no deterrents. We walked a mile down Beaver Dam Canyon, then climbed the western slope. As long as the sun shone I knew the country fairly well, or rather my direction. We slipped along through the silent woods, satisfied with everything. Presently the sun broke through the clouds, and shone fitfully, making intervals of shadow, and others of golden-green verdure.

Along an edge of one of the grassy parks we came across fresh deer tracks. Several deer had run out of the woods just ahead of us, evidently having winded us. One track was that of a big buck. We trailed these tracks across the park, then made a detour in hopes of heading the deer off, but failed. A huge, dark cloud scudded out of the west and let down a shower of fine rain. We kept dry under a spreading spruce. The forest then was gloomy and cool with only a faint moan of wind and pattering of raindrops to break the silence. The cloud passed by, the sun shone again, the forest glittered in its dress of diamonds. There had been but little frost, so that aspen and maple thickets had not yet taken on their cloth of gold and blaze of red. Most of the leaves were still on the trees, making these thickets impossible to see into. We hunted along the edges of these, and across the wide, open ridge from canyon to canyon, and saw nothing but old tracks. Black and white clouds rolled up and brought a squall. We

took to another spruce tent for shelter. After this squall the
sky became obscured by a field of gray cloud through which
the sun shone dimly. This matter worried me. I was aware of
my direction then, but if I lost the sun I would soon be in
difficulties.

Gradually we worked back along the ridge toward camp,
and headed several ravines that ran and widened down into
the big canyon. All at once R. C. held up a warning finger.
"Listen!" With abatement of breath I listened, but heard
nothing except the mournful sough of the pines. "Thought I
heard a whistle," he said. We went on, all eyes and ears.

R. C. and I flattered ourselves that together we made rather
a good hunting team. We were fairly well versed in woodcraft
and could slip along stealthily. I possessed an Indian sense of
direction that had never yet failed me. To be sure we had
much to learn about deer stalking. But I had never hunted with
any man whose ears were as quick as R. C.'s. A naturally
keen hearing, and many years of still hunting, accounted for
this faculty. As for myself, the one gift of which I was
especially proud was my eyesight. Almost invariably I could
see game in the woods before any one who was with me. This
had applied to all my guides except Indians. And I believed
that five summers on the Pacific, searching the wide expanse
of ocean for swordfish fins, had made my eyes all the keener
for the woods. R. C. and I played at a game in which he tried
to hear the movement of some forest denizen before I saw it.
This fun for us dated back to boyhood days.

Suddenly R. C. stopped short, with his head turning to one
side, and his body stiffening. "I heard that whistle again," he
said. We stood perfectly motionless for a long moment. Then
from far off in the forest I heard a high, clear, melodious,
bugling note. How thrilling, how lonely a sound!

"It's a bull-elk," I replied. Then we sat down upon a log
and listened. R. C. had heard that whistle in Colorado, but
had not recognized it. Just as the mournful howl of a wolf is
the wildest, most haunting sound of the wilderness, so is the
bugle of the elk the noblest, most melodious and thrilling.
With tingling nerves and strained ears we listened. We heard
elk bugling in different directions, hard to locate. One bull

appeared to be low down, another high up, another working away. R. C. and I decided to stalk them. The law prohibited the killing of elk, but that was no reason why we might not trail them, and have the sport of seeing them in their native haunts. So we stole softly through the woods, halting now and then to listen, pleased to note that every whistle we heard appeared to be closer.

At last, apparently only a deep thicketed ravine separated us from the ridge upon which the elk were bugling. Here our stalk began to become really exciting. We did not make any noise threading that wet thicket, and we ascended the opposite slope very cautiously. What little wind there was blew from the elk toward us, so they could not scent us. Once up on the edge of the ridge we halted to listen. After a long time we heard a far-away bugle, then another at least half a mile distant. Had we miscalculated? R. C. was for working down the ridge and I was for waiting there a few moments. So we sat down again. The forest was almost silent now. Somewhere a squirrel was barking. The sun peeped out of the pale clouds, lighted the glades, rimmed the pines in brightness. I opened my lips to speak to R. C. when I was rendered mute by a piercing whistle, high-pitched and sweet and melodiously prolonged. It made my ears tingle and my blood dance. "Right close," whispered R. C. "Come on." We began to steal through the forest, keeping behind trees and thickets, peeping out, and making no more sound than shadows. The ground was damp, facilitating our noiseless stalk. In this way we became separated by about thirty steps, but we walked on and halted in unison. Passing through a thicket of little pines we came into an open forest full of glades. Keenly I peered everywhere, as I slipped from tree to tree. Finally we stooped along for a space, and then, at a bugle blast so close that it made me jump, I began to crawl. My objective point was a fallen pine the trunk of which appeared high enough to conceal me. R. C. kept working a little farther to the right. Once he beckoned me, but I kept on. Still I saw him drop down to crawl. Our stalk was getting toward its climax. My state was one of quivering intensity of thrill, of excitement, of pleasure. Reaching my log I peeped over it. I saw a cow-elk and a yearling calf trotting across a glade about a hundred yards distant. Wanting R. C. to see them I looked his way, and pointed. But he was pointing also and vehemently beckoning for me to join him. I ran on all fours over to where he knelt. He whispered pantingly: "Grandest sight—ever saw!" I peeped out.

In a glade not seventy-five yards away stood a magnificent bull elk, looking back over his shoulder. His tawny hind-quarters, then his dark brown, almost black shaggy shoulders and head, then his enormous spread of antlers, like the top of a dead cedar—these in turn fascinated my gaze. How graceful, stately, lordly!

R. C. stepped out from behind the pine in full view. I crawled out, took a kneeling position, and drew a bead on the elk. I had the fun of imagining I could have hit him any-where. I did not really want to kill him, yet what was the meaning of the sharp, hot gush of my blood, the fiery thrill along my nerves, the feeling of unsatisfied wildness? The bull eyed us for a second, then laid his forest of antlers back over his shoulders, and with singularly swift, level stride, sped like a tawny flash into the green forest.

R. C. and I began to chatter like boys, and to walk toward the glade, without any particular object in mind, when my roving eye caught sight of a moving brown and checkered patch low down on the ground, vanishing behind a thicket. I called R. C. and ran. I got to where I could see beyond the thicket. An immense flock of turkeys! I yelled. As I tried to get a bead on a running turkey R. C. joined me. "Chase 'em!" he yelled. So we dashed through the forest with the turkeys running ahead of us. Never did they come out clear in the open. I halted to shoot, but just as I was about to press the trigger my moving target vanished. This happened again. No use to shoot at random! I had a third fleeting chance, but absolutely could not grasp it. Then the big flock of turkeys eluded us in an impenetrable brushy ravine.

"By George!" exclaimed R. C. "Can you beat that? They run like streaks. I couldn't aim. These wild turkeys are great."

I echoed his sentiments. We prowled around for an hour trying to locate this flock again, but all in vain. "Well," said

R. C. finally, as he wiped his perspiring face, "it's good to see some game anyhow. . . . Where are we?"

It developed that our whereabouts was a mystery to me. The sun had become completely obliterated, a fine rain was falling, the forest had grown wet and dismal. We had gotten turned around. The matter did not look serious, however, until we had wandered around for another hour without finding anything familiar. Then we realized we were lost. This sort of experience had happened to R. C. and me often; nevertheless we did not relish it, especially the first day out. As usual on such occasions R. C. argued with me about direction, and then left the responsibility with me. I found an open spot, somewhat sheltered on one side from the misty rain, and there I stationed myself to study trees and sky and clouds for some clue to help me decide what was north or west. After a while I had the good fortune to see a momentary brightening through the clouds. I located the sun, and was pleased to discover that the instinct of direction I had been subtly prompted to take would have helped me as much as the sun.

We faced east and walked fast, and I took note of trees ahead so that we should not get off a straight line. At last we came to a deep canyon. In the gray misty rain I could not be sure I recognized it. "Well, R. C.," I said, "this may be our canyon, and it may not. But to make sure we'll follow it up to the rim. Then we can locate camp." R. C. replied with weary disdain. "All right, my redskin brother, lead me to camp. As Loren says, I'm starved to death." Loren is my three-year-old boy, who bids fair to be like his brother Romer. He has an enormous appetite and before meal times he complains bitterly: "I'm starv-ved to death!" How strange to remember him while I was lost in the forest!

When we had descended into the canyon rain was falling more heavily. We were in for it. But I determined we would not be kept out all night. So I struck forward with long stride.

In half an hour we came to where the canyon forked. I deliberated a moment. Not one familiar landmark could I descry, from which fact I decided we had better take to the left-hand fork. Grass and leaves appeared almost as wet as running water. Soon we were soaked to the skin. After two miles the canyon narrowed and thickened, so that traveling grew more and more laborsome. It must have been four miles from its mouth to where it headed up near the rim. Once out of it we found ourselves on familiar ground, about five miles from camp. Exhausted and wet and nearly frozen we reached camp just before dark. If I had taken the right-hand fork of the canyon, which was really Beaver Dam Canyon, we would have gotten back to camp in short order. R. C. said to the boys: "Well, Doc dragged me nine miles out of our way." Everybody but the Jap enjoyed my discomfiture. Takahashi said in his imperfect English: "Go get on more better dry clothes. Soon hot supper. Maybe good yes!"

V

It rained the following day, making a good excuse to stay in camp and rest beside the little tent-stove. And the next morning I started out on foot with Copple. We went down Beaver Dam Canyon intending to go up on the ridge where R. C. and I had seen the flock of turkeys.

I considered Copple an addition to my long list of outdoor acquaintances in the west, and believed him a worthy partner for Nielsen. Copple was born near Oak Creek, some twenty miles south of Flagstaff, and was one-fourth Indian. He had a good education. His whole life had been in the open, which fact I did not need to be told. A cowboy when only a boy he had also been sheepherder, miner, freighter, and everything Arizonian. Eighteen years he had hunted game and prospected for gold in Mexico. He had been a sailor and fireman on the Pacific, he had served in the army in the Philippines. Altogether his had been an adventurous life; and as Doyle had been a mine of memories for me so would Copple be a mine of information. Such men have taught me the wonder, the violence, the truth of the west.

Copple was inclined to be loquacious—a trait that ordinarily was rather distasteful to me, but in his case would be an advantage. On our way down the canyon not only did he give me an outline of the history of his life, but he talked about how he had foretold the storm just ended. The fresh diggings of gophers—little mounds of dirt thrown up—had indicated the approach of the storm; so had the hooting of owls; likewise the twittering of snowbirds at that season; also the feeding of blackbirds near horses. Particularly a wind from the south meant storm. From that he passed to a discussion of deer. During the light of the moon deer feed at night; and in the day time they will lie in a thicket. If a hunter came near the deer would lower their horns flat and remain motionless, unless almost ridden over. In the dark of the moon deer feed at early morning, lie down during the day, and feed again toward sunset, always alert, trusting to nose more than eyes and ears.

Copple was so interesting that I must have passed the place where R. C. and I had come down into the canyon; at any rate I missed it, and we went on farther. Copple showed me old bear sign, an old wolf track, and then fresh turkey tracks. The latter reminded me that we were out hunting. I could carry a deadly rifle in my hands, yet dream dreams of flower-decked Elysian fields. We climbed a wooded bench or low step of the canyon slope, and though Copple and I were side by side I saw two turkeys before he did. They were running swiftly up hill. I took a snap shot at the lower one, but missed. My bullet struck low, upsetting him. Both of them disappeared.

Then we climbed to the top of the ridge, and in scouting around along the heavily timbered edges we came to a ravine deep enough to be classed as a canyon. Here the forest was dark and still, with sunlight showing down in rays and gleams. While hunting I always liked to sit down here and there to listen and watch. Copple liked this too. So we sat down. Opposite us the rocky edge of the other slope was about two hundred yards. We listened to jays and squirrels. I made note of the significant fact that as soon as we began to hunt Copple became silent.

Presently my roving eye caught sight of a moving object. It is movement that always attracts my eye in the woods. I saw a plump, woolly beast walk out upon the edge of the opposite slope and stand in the shade.

"Copple, is that a sheep?" I whispered, pointing. "Lion—no, big lynx," he replied. I aimed and shot just a little too swiftly. Judging by the puff of dust my bullet barely missed the big cat. He leaped fully fifteen feet. Copple fired, hitting right under his nose as he alighted. That whirled him back. He bounced like a rubber ball. My second shot went over him, and Copple's hit between his legs. Then with another prodigious bound he disappeared in a thicket. 'By golly! we missed him," declared Copple. "But you must have shaved him that first time. Biggest lynx I ever saw."

We crossed the canyon and hunted for him, but without success. Then we climbed an open grassy forest slope, up to a level ridge, and crossed that to see down into a beautiful valley, with stately isolated pines, and patches of aspens, and floor of luxuriant grass. A ravine led down into this long park and the mouth of it held a thicket of small pines. Just as we got half way out I saw bobbing black objects above the high grass. I peered sharply. These objects were turkey heads. I got a shot before Copple saw them. There was a bouncing, a whirring, a thumping—and then turkeys appeared to be running every way.

Copple fired. "Turkey number one!" he called out. I missed a big gobbler on the run. Copple shot again. "Turkey number two!" he called out. I could not see what he had done, but of course I knew he had done execution. It roused my ire as well as a desperate ambition. Turkeys were running up hill everywhere. I aimed at this one, then at that. Again I fired. Another miss! How that gobbler ran! He might just as well have flown. Every turkey contrived to get a tree or bush between him and me, just at the critical instant. In despair I tried to hold on the last one, got a bead on it through my peep sight, moved it with him as we moved, and holding tight, I fired. With a great flop and scattering of bronze feathers he went down. I ran up the slope and secured him, a fine gobbler of about fifteen pounds weight.

Upon my return to Copple I found he had collected his two turkeys, both shot in the neck in the same place. He said: "If you hit them in the body you spoil them for cooking. I used to hit all mine in the head. Let me give you a hunch. Always pick out a turkey running straight away from you or straight toward you. Never crossways. You can't hit them running to the side."

Then he bluntly complimented me upon my eyesight. That at least was consolation for my poor shooting. We rested there, and after a while heard a turkey cluck. Copple had no turkey-caller, but he clucked anyhow. We heard answers. The flock evidently was trying to get together again, and some of them were approaching us. Copple continued to call. Then I appreciated how fascinating R. C. had found this calling game. Copple got answers from all around, growing closer. But presently the answers ceased. "They're on to me," he whispered and did not call again. At that moment a young gobbler ran swiftly down the slope and stopped to peer around, his long neck stretching. It was not a very long shot, and I, scorning to do less than Copple, tried to emulate him, and aimed at the neck of the gobbler. All I got, however, was a few feathers. Like a grouse he flew across the opening and was gone. We lingered there a while, hoping to see or hear more of the flock, but did neither. Copple tried to teach me how to tell the age of turkeys from their feet, a lesson I did not think I would assimilate in one hunting season. He tied their legs together and hung them over his shoulder, a net weight of about fifty pounds.

All the way up that valley we saw elk tracks, and once from over the ridge I heard a bugle. On our return toward camp we followed a rather meandering course, over ridge and down dale, and through grassy parks and stately forests, and along the slowly coloring maple-aspen thickets. Copple claimed to hear deer running, but I did not. Many tired footsteps I dragged along before we finally reached Beaver Dam Canyon. How welcome the sight of camp! R. C. had ridden miles with Edd, and had seen one deer that they said was still enjoying his freedom in the woods. Takahashi hailed sight of the turkeys with: "That fine! That fine! Nice fat ones!"

But tired as I was that night I still had enthusiasm enough to visit Haught's camp, and renew acquaintance with the hounds. Haught had not been able to secure more than two new hounds, and these named Rock and Buck were still unknown quantities.

Old Dan remembered me, and my heart warmed to the old gladiator. He was a very big, large-boned hound, gray with age and wrinkled and lame, and bleary-eyed. Dan was too old to be put on trails, or at least to be made chase bear. He loved a camp-fire, and would almost sit in the flames. This fact, and the way he would beg for a morsel to eat, had endeared him to me.

Old Tom was somewhat smaller and leaner than Dan, yet resembled him enough to deceive us at times. Tom was gray, too, and had crinkly ears, and many other honorable battle-scars. Tom was not quite so friendly as Dan; in fact he had more dignity. Still neither hound was ever demonstrative except upon sight of his master. Haught told me that if Dan and Tom saw him shoot at a deer they would chase it till they dropped; accordingly he never shot at anything except bear and lion when he had these hounds with him.

Sue was the best hound in the pack, as she still had, in spite of years of service, a good deal of speed and fight left in her. She was a slim, dark brown hound with fine and very long ears. Rock, one of the new hounds from Kentucky, was white and black, and had remarkably large, clear and beautiful eyes, almost human in expression. I could not account for the fact that I suspected Rock was a deer chaser. Buck, the other hound from Kentucky, was no longer young; he had a stump tail; his color was a little yellow with dark spots, and he had a hang-dog head and distrustful eye. I made certain that Buck had never had any friends, for he did not understand kindness. Nor had he ever had enough to eat. He stayed away from the rest of the pack and growled fiercely when a pup came near him. I tried to make friends with him, but found that I would not have an easy task.

Kaiser Bill was one of the pups, black in color, a long, lean, hungry-looking dog, and crazy. He had not grown any in a year, either in body or intelligence. I remembered how he would yelp just to hear himself and run any kind of a trail— how he would be the first to quit and come back. And if any one fired a gun near him he would run like a scared deer.

To be fair to Kaiser Bill the other pups were not much better. Trailer and Big Foot were young still, and about all they could do was to run and howl.

If, however, they got off right on a bear trail, and no other trail crossed it they would stick, and in fact lead the pack till the bear got away. Once Big Foot came whimpering into camp with porcupine quills in his nose. Of all the whipped and funny pups!

Bobby was the dog I liked best. He was a curly black half-shepherd, small in size; and he had a sharp, intelligent face, with the brightest hazel eyes. His manner of wagging his tail seemed most comical yet convincing. Bobby wagged only the nether end and that most emphatically. He would stand up to me, holding out his forepaws, and beg. What an appealing beggar he was! Bobby's value to Haught was not inconsiderable. He was the only dog Haught ever had that would herd the pigs. On a bear hunt Bobby lost his shepherd ways and his kindly disposition, and yelped fiercely, and hung on a trail as long as any of the pack. He had no fear of a bear, for which reason Haught did not like to run him.

All told then we had a rather nondescript and poor pack of hounds; and the fact discouraged me. I wanted to hunt the bad cinnamons and the grizzly sheep-killers, with which this rim-rock country was infested. I had nothing against the acorn-eating brown or black bears. And with this pack of hounds I doubted that we could hold one of the vicious fighting species. But there was now nothing to do but try. No one could tell. We might kill a big grizzly. And the fact that the chances were against us perhaps made for more determined effort. I regretted, however, that I had not secured a pack of trained hounds somewhere.

Frost was late this fall. The acorns had hardly ripened, the leaves had scarcely colored; and really good bear hunting seemed weeks off. A storm and then a cold snap would help matters wonderfully, and for these we hoped. Indeed the weather had not settled; hardly a day had been free of clouds. But despite conditions we decided to start in bear hunting every other day, feeling that at least we could train the pack, and get them and ourselves in better shape for a favorable time when it arrived.

Accordingly next day we sallied forth for Horton Thicket, and I went down with Edd and George. It was a fine day, sunny and windy at intervals. The new trail the boys had made was boggy. From above Horton Thicket looked dark, green, verdant, with scarcely any touch of autumn colors; from below, once in it, all seemed a darker green, cool and damp. Water lay in all low places. The creek roared bankfull of clear water.

The new trail led up and down over dark red rich earth, through thickets of jack-pine and maple, and then across long slopes of manzanita and juniper, mescal and oak. Junipers were not fruitful this year as they were last, only a few having clusters of lavender-colored berries. The manzanita brush appeared exceptionally beautiful with its vivid contrasts of crimson and green leaves, orange-colored berries, and smooth, shiny bark of a chocolate red. The mescal consisted of round patches of cactus with spear-shaped leaves, low on the ground, with a long dead stalk standing or broken down. This stalk grows fresh every spring, when it is laden with beautiful yellow blossoms. The honey from the flowers of mescal and mesquite is the best to be obtained in this country of innumerable bees.

Presently the hounds opened up on some kind of a trail and they worked on it around under the ledges toward the next canyon, called See Canyon. After a while the country grew so rough that fast riding was impossible; the thickets tore and clutched at us until they finally stopped the horses. We got off. Edd climbed to a ridge-top. "Pack gone way round," he called. "I'll walk. Take my horse back." I decided to let George take my horse also, and I hurried to catch up with Edd.

Following that long-legged Arizonian on foot was almost as strenuous as keeping him in sight on horseback. I managed it. We climbed steep slopes and the farther we climbed the thicker grew the brush. Often we would halt to listen for hounds, at which welcome intervals I endeavored to catch my breath. We kept the hounds in hearing, which fact incited us to renewed endeavors. At length we got into a belt of live-oak and scrub-pine brush, almost as difficult to penetrate as manzanita, and here we had to bend and crawl. Bear and deer tracks led everywhere. Small stones and large stones had been lifted and displaced by bears searching for grubs. These slopes were dry; we found no water at the heads of ravines, yet the red earth was rich in bearded, tufted grass, yellow daisies and purple asters, and a wan blue flower. We climbed and climbed, until my back began to give me trouble. "Reckon we—bit off—a big hunk," remarked Edd once, and I thought he referred to the endless steep and brushy slopes. By and bye the hounds came back to us one by one, all footsore and weary. Manifestly the bear had outrun them. Our best prospect then was to climb on to the rim and strike across the forest to camp.

I noticed that tired as I was I had less trouble to keep up with Edd. His boots wore very slippery on grass and pine-needles, so that he might have been trying to climb on ice. I had nails in my boots and they caught hold. Hotter and wetter I grew until I had a burning sensation all over. My legs and arms ached; the rifle weighed a ton; my feet seemed to take hold of the ground and stick. We could not go straight up owing to the nature of that jumble of broken cliffs and matted scrub forests. For hours we toiled onward, upward, downward, and then upward. Only through such experience could I have gained an adequate knowledge of the roughness and vastness of this rim-rock country.

At last we arrived at the base of the gray leaning crags, and there, on a long slide of weathered rock the hounds jumped a bear. I saw the dust he raised, as he piled into the thicket below the slide. What a wild clamor from the hounds! We got out on the rocky slope where we could see and kept sharp eyes roving, but the bear went straight down hill. Amazing indeed was it the way the hounds drew away from us. In a few moments they were at the foot of the slopes, tearing back over the course we had been so many hours in coming. Then we set out to get on the rim, so as to follow along it, and keep track of the chase. Edd distanced me on the rocks. I had to stop often. My breast labored and I could scarcely breathe. I sweat so freely that my rifle stock was wet. My hardest battle was in fighting a tendency to utter weariness and disgust. My old poignant feelings about my physical condition returned to vex me. As a matter of fact I had already that very day accomplished a climb not at all easy for the Arizonian, and I should have been happy. But I had not been used to a lame back. When I reached the rim I fell there, and lay there a few moments, until I could get up. Then I followed along after Edd whose yells to the hounds I heard, and overtook him upon the point of a promontory. Far below the hounds were baying. "They're chasin' him all right," declared Edd, grimly. "He's headin' for low country. I think Sue stopped him once. But the rest of the pack are behind."

I had never been on the point of this promontory. Grand indeed was the panorama. Under me yawned a dark-green, smoky-canyoned, rippling basin of timber and red rocks leading away to the mountain ranges of the Four Peaks and Mazatzals. Westward, toward the yellowing sunset stood out long escarpments for miles, and long sloping lines of black ridges, leading down to the basin where there seemed to be a ripple of the earth, a vast upset region of canyon and ridge, wild and lonely and dark.

I did not get to see the sunset from that wonderful point, a matter I regretted. We were far from camp, and Edd was not sure of a bee-line during daylight, let alone after dark. Deep in the forest the sunset gold and red burned on grass and leaf. The aspens took most of the color. Swift-flying wisps of cloud turned pink, and low along the wester horizon of the forest the light seemed golden and blue.

I was almost exhausted, and by the time we reached camp, just at dark, I was wholly exhausted. My voice had sunk to a whisper, a fact that occasioned R. C. some concern until I could explain. Undoubtedly this was the hardest day's work I had done since my lion hunting with Buffalo Jones. It did not surprise me that next day I had to forget my crosscut saw exercise.

Late that afternoon the hounds came straggling into camp, lame and starved. Sue was the last one in, arriving at supper-time.

Another day found me still sore, but able to ride, and R. C. and I went off into the woods in search of any kind of adventure. This day was cloudy and threatening, with spells of sunshine. We saw two bull elk, a cow and a calf. The bulls

appeared remarkably agile for so heavy an animal. Neither of
these, however, were of such magnificent proportions as the
one R. C. and I had stalked the first day out. A few minutes
later we scared out three more cows and three yearlings. I
dismounted just for fun, and sighted my rifle at four of them.
Next we came to a canyon where beaver had cut aspen trees.
These animals must have chisel-like teeth. They left chip-
pings somewhat similar to those cut by an axe. Aspen bark
was their winter food. In this particular spot we could not find
a dam or slide. When we rode down into Turkey Canyon,
however, we found a place where beavers had dammed the
brook. Many aspens were fresh cut, one at least two feet
thick, and all the small branches had been cut off and dragged
to the water, where I could find no further trace of them. The
grass was matted down, and on the bare bits of ground
showed beaver tracks.

Game appeared to be scarce. Haught had told us that deer,
turkey and bear had all gone to feed on the mast (fallen
acorns); and if we could locate the mast we would find the
game. He said he had once seen a herd of several hundred
deer migrating from one section of country to another. Apparently this was to find new feeding grounds.

While we were resting under a spruce I espied a white-
breasted, blue-headed, gray-backed little bird at work on a
pine tree. He walked head first down the bark, pecking here
and there. I saw a moth or a winged insect fly off the tree,
and then another. Then I saw several more fly away. The bird
was feeding on winged insects that lived in the bark. Some of
them saw or heard him coming and escaped, but many of them
he caught. He went about this death-dealing business with a
brisk and cheerful manner. No doubt nature had developed him
to help protect the trees from bugs and worms and beetles.

Later that day, in an open grassy canyon, we came upon
quite a large bird, near the size of a pigeon, which I thought
appeared to be a species of jay or magpie. This bird had gray
and black colors, a round head, and a stout bill. At first I
thought it was crippled, as it hopped and fluttered about in the
grass. I got down to catch it. Then I discovered it was only
tame. I could approach to within a foot of reaching it. Once it

perched upon a low snag, and peeped at me with little bright
dark eyes, very friendly, as if he liked my company. I sat
there within a few feet of him for quite a while. We resumed
our ride. Crossing a fresh buck track caused us to dismount,
and tie our horses. But that buck was too wary for us. We
returned to camp as usual, empty handed as far as game was
concerned.

I forgot to say anything to Haught or Doyle about the black
and gray bird that had so interested me. Quite a coincidence
was it then to see another such bird and that one right in
camp. He appeared to be as tame as the other. He flew and
hopped around camp in such a friendly manner that I placed a
piece of meat in a conspicuous place for him. Not long was
he in finding it. He alighted on it, and pecked and pulled at a
great rate. Doyle claimed it was a Clark crow, named after
one of the Lewis and Clark expedition. "It's a rare bird,"
said Doyle. "First one I've seen in thirty years." As Doyle
spent most of his time in the open this statement seemed rather
remarkable.

We had frost on two mornings, temperature as low as twenty-
six degrees, and then another change indicative of unsettled
weather. It rained, and sleeted, and then snowed, but the
ground was too wet to hold the snow.

The wilderness began all at once, as if by magic, to take on
autumn colors. Then the forest became an enchanted region
of white aspens, golden-green aspens, purple spruces, dark
green pines, maples a blaze of vermilion, cerise, scarlet,
magenta, rose—and slopes of dull red sumac. These were the
beginning of Indian summer days, the melancholy days, with
their color and silence and beauty and fragrance and mystery.

Hunting then became quite a dream for me, as if it called
back to me dim mystic days in the woods of some past weird
world. One afternoon Copple, R. C., and I went as far as the
east side of Gentry Canyon and worked down. Copple found
fresh deer and turkey sign. We tied our horses, and slipped
back against the wind. R. C. took one side of a ridge, with
Copple and me on the other, and we worked down toward
where we had seen the sign. After half an hour of slow,
stealthy glide through the forest we sat down at the edge of a

park, expecting R. C. to come along soon. The white aspens were all bare, and oak leaves were rustling down. The wind lulled a while, then softly roared in the pines. All at once both of us heard a stick crack, and light steps of a walking deer on leaves. Copple whispered: "Get ready to shoot." We waited, keen and tight, expecting to see a deer walk out into the open. But none came. Leaving our stand we slipped into the woods, careful not to make the slightest sound. Such careful, slow steps were certainly not accountable for the rapid beat of my heart. Something gray moved among the green and yellow leaves. I halted, and held Copple back. Then not twenty paces away I descried what I thought was a fawn. It glided toward us without the slightest sound. Suddenly, half emerging from some maple saplings, it saw us and seemed stricken to stone. Not ten steps from me! Soft gray hue, slender graceful neck and body, sleek small head with long ears, and great dark distended eyes, wilder than any wild eyes I had ever beheld. I saw it quiver all over. I was quivering too, but with emotion. Copple whispered: "Yearlin' buck. Shoot!"

His whisper, low as it was, made the deer leap like a gray flash. Also it broke the spell for me. "Year old buck!" I exclaimed, quite loud. "Thought he was a fawn. But I couldn't have shot——"

A crash of brush interrupted me. Thump of hoofs, crack of branches—then a big buck deer bounded onward into the thicket. I got one snap shot at his fleeting blurred image and missed him. We ran ahead, but to no avail.

"Four-point buck," said Copple. "He must have been standin' behind that brush."

"Did you see his horns?" I gasped, incredulously.

"Sure. But he was runnin' some. Let's go down this slope where he jumped. . . . Now will you look at that! Here's where he started after you shot."

A gentle slope, rather open, led down to the thicket where the buck had vanished. We measured the first of his downhill jumps, and it amounted to eighteen of my rather short steps. What a magnificent leap! It reminded me of the story of Hart-leap Well.

As we retraced our steps R. C. met us, reporting that he had heard the buck running, but could not see him. We scouted around together for an hour, then R. C. and Copple started off on a wide detour, leaving me at a stand in the hope they might drive some turkeys my way. I sat on a log until almost sunset. All the pine tips turned gold and patches of gold brightened the ground. Jays were squalling, gray squirrels were barking, red squirrels were chattering, snowbirds were twittering, pine cones were dropping, leaves were rustling. But there were no turkeys, and I did not miss them. R. C. and Copple returned to tell me there were signs of turkeys and deer all over the ridge. "We'll ride over here early to-morrow," said Copple, "an' I'll bet my gun we pack some meat to camp."

But the unsettled weather claimed the next day and the next, giving us spells of rain and sleet, and periods of sunshine deceptive in their promise. Camp, however, with our big camp-fire, and little tent-stoves, and Takahashi, would have been delightful in almost any weather. Takahashi was insulted, the boys told me, because I said he was born to be a cook. It seemed the Jap looked down upon this culinary job. "Cook—that woman joob!" he said, contemptuously.

As I became better acquainted with Takahashi I learned to think more of the Japanese. I studied Takahashi very earnestly and I grew to like him. The Orientals are mystics and hard to understand. But any one could see that here was a Japanese who was a real man. I never saw him idle. He resented being told what to do, and after my first offense in this regard I never gave him another order. He was a wonderful cook. It pleased his vanity to see how good an appetite I always had. When I would hail him: "George, what you got to eat?" he would grin and reply: "Aw, turkee!" Then I would let out a yell, for I never in my life tasted anything so good as the roast wild turkey Takahashi served us. Or he would say: "Pan-cakes—apple dumplings—rice puddings." No one but the Japs know how to cook rice. I asked him how he cooked rice over an open fire and he said: "I know how hot—when done." Takahashi must have possessed an uncanny knowledge of the effects of heat. How swift, clean, efficient and saving he was! He never wasted anything. In these days of American prodigality a frugal cook like Takahashi was a revelation. Seldom are the real producers of food ever wasters. Takahashi's ambition was to be a rancher in California. I learned many things about him. In summer he went to the Imperial Valley where he picked and packed cantaloupes. He could stand the intense heat. He was an expert. He commanded the highest wage. Then he was a raisin-picker, which for him was another art. He had accumulated a little fortune and knew how to save his money. He would have been a millionaire in Japan, but he intended to live in the United States.

Takahashi had that best of traits—generosity. Whenever he made pie or cake or doughnuts he always saved his share for me to have for my lunch next day. No use to try to break him of this kindly habit! He was keen too, and held in particular disfavor any one who picked out the best portions of turkey or meat. "No like that," he would say; and I heartily agreed with him. Life in the open brought out the little miserable traits of human nature, of which no one was absolutely free.

I admired Takahashi's cooking, I admired the enormous pile of firewood he always had chopped, I admired his generosity; but most of all I liked his cheerfulness and good humor. He grew to be a joy to me. We had some pop corn which we sometimes popped over the campfire. He was fond of it and he said: "You eat all time—much pop corn—just so long you keep mouth going all same like horse—you happy." We were troubled a good deal by skunks. Now some skunks were not bad neighbors, but others were disgusting and dangerous. The hog-nosed skunk, according to westerners, very often had hydrophobia and would bite a sleeper. I knew of several men dying of rabies from this bite. Copple said he had been awakened twice at night by skunks biting the noses of his companions in camp. Copple had to choke the skunks off. One of these men died. We were really afraid of them. Doyle said one had visited him in his tent and he had been forced to cover his head until he nearly smothered. Now Takahashi slept in the tent with the store of supplies. One night a skunk awakened him. In reporting this to me the Jap said: "See skunk all black and white at tent door. I flash light. Skunk no 'fraid. He no run. He act funny—then just walk off.''

After that experience Takahashi set a box-trap for skunks. One morning he said with a huge grin: ''I catch skunk. Want you take picture for me send my wife Sadayo.''

So I got my camera, and being careful to take a safe position, as did all the boys, I told Takahashi I was ready to photograph him and his skunk. He got a pole that was too short to suit me, and he lifted up the box-trap. A furry white and black cat appeared, with remarkably bushy tail. What a beautiful little animal to bear such opprobrium! ''All same like cat,'' said Takahashi. ''Kittee—kittee.'' It appeared that kitty was not in the least afraid. On the contrary she surveyed the formidable Jap with his pole, and her other enemies in a calm, dignified manner. Then she turned away. Here I tried to photograph her and Takahashi together. When she started off the Jap followed and poked her with the pole. ''Take 'nother picture.'' But kitty suddenly whirled, with fur and tail erect, a most surprising and brave and assured front, then ran at Takahashi. I yelled: ''Run George!'' Pell-mell everybody fled from that beautiful little beast. We were arrant cowards. But Takahashi grasped up another and longer pole, and charged back at kitty. This time he chased her out of camp. When he returned his face was a study: ''Nashty thing! She make awful stink! She no 'fraid a tall. Next time I kill her sure!''

The head of Gentry Canyon was about five miles from camp, and we reached it the following morning while the frost was still white and sparkling. We tied our horses. Copple said: ''This is a deer day. I'll show you a buck sure. Let's stick together an' walk easy.''

So we made sure to work against the wind, which, however, was so light as almost to be imperceptible, and stole along the dark ravine, taking half a dozen steps or so at a time. How still the forest! When it was like this I always felt as if I had discovered something new. The big trees loomed stately and calm, stretching a rugged network of branches over us. Fortunately no saucy squirrels or squalling jays appeared to be abroad to warn game of our approach. Not only a tang, but a thrill, seemed to come pervasively on the cool air. All the colors of autumn were at their height, and gorgeous plots of maple thicket and sumac burned against the brown and green. We slipped along, each of us strung to be the first to hear or see some living creature of the wild. R. C., as might have been expected, halted us with a softly whispered: "Listen." But neither Copple nor I heard what R. C. heard, and presently we moved on as before. Presently again R. C. made us pause, with a like result. Somehow the forest seemed unusually wild. It provoked a tingling expectation. The pine-covered slope ahead of us, the thicketed ridge to our left, the dark, widening ravine to our right, all seemed to harbor listening, watching, soft-footed denizens of the wild. At length we reached a level bench, beautifully forested, where the ridge ran down in points to where the junction of several ravines formed the head of Gentry Canyon.

How stealthily we stole on! Here Copple said was a place for deer to graze. But the grass plots, golden with sunlight and white with frost and black-barred by shadows of pines, showed no game.

Copple sat down on a log, and I took a seat beside him to the left. R. C. stood just to my left. As I laid my rifle over my knees and opened my lips to whisper I was suddenly struck mute. I saw R. C. stiffen, then crouch a little. He leaned forward—his eyes had the look of a falcon. Then I distinctly heard the soft crack of hoofs on stone and breaking of tiny twigs. Quick as I whirled my head I still caught out of the tail of my eye the jerk of R. C. as he threw up his rifle. I looked—I strained my eyes—I flashed them along the rim of the ravine where R. C. had been gazing. A gray form seemed to move into the field of my vision. That instant it leaped, and R. C.'s rifle shocked me with its bursting crack. I seemed stunned, so near was the report. But I saw the gray form pitch headlong and I heard a solid thump.

"Buck, an' he's your meat!" called Copple, low and sharp. "Look for another one."

No other deer appeared. R. C. ran toward the spot where the gray form had plunged in a heap, and Copple and I followed. It was far enough to make me pant for breath. We found R. C. beside a fine three-point buck that had been shot

square in the back of the head between and below the roots of
its antlers.

"Never knew what struck him!" exclaimed Copple, and he
laid hold of the deer and hauled it out of the edge of the
thicket. "Fine an' fat. Venison for camp, boys. One of you
go after the horses an' the other help me hang him up."

VI

I had been riding eastward of Beaver Dam Canyon with
Haught, and we had parted up on the ridge, he to go down a
ravine leading to his camp, and I to linger a while longer up
there in the Indian-summer woods, so full of gold and silence
and fragrance on that October afternoon.

The trail gradually drew me onward and downward, and at
length I came out into a narrow open park lined by spruce
trees. Suddenly Don Carlos shot up his ears. I had not ridden
him for days and he appeared more than usually spirited. He
saw or heard something. I held him in, and after a moment I
dismounted and drew my rifle. A crashing in brush somewhere near at hand excited me. Peering all around I tried to
locate cause for the sound. Again my ear caught a violent
swishing of brush accompanied by a snapping of twigs. This
time I cocked my rifle. Don Carlos snorted. After another
circling swift gaze it dawned upon me that the sound came
from overhead.

I looked into this tree and that, suddenly to have my gaze
arrested by a threshing commotion in the very top of a lofty
spruce. I saw a dark form moving against a background of
blue sky. Instantly I thought it must be a lynx and was about
to raise my rifle when a voice as from the very clouds utterly
astounded me. I gasped in my astonishment. Was I dreaming?
But violent threshings and whacks from the tree-top absolutely assured me that I was neither dreaming nor out of my
head. "I get you—whee!" shouted the voice. There was a
man up in the swaying top of that spruce and he was no other
than Takahashi. For a moment I could not find my voice.
Then I shouted:

"Hey up there, George! What in the world are you doing?
I came near shooting you."

Zane Grey looking over the Tonto Basin from the Mogollon Rim.

Romer Grey on horseback, ready for the hunt.

Looking toward the snow-capped peaks.

Grey's camp in the Tonto Basin.

R. C. Grey and his wife, Reba, riding with one of the hounds.

The author and his guides in the Tonto Basin. Left to right: Edd Haught, Nielsen, Babe Haught (the bear hunter), Al Doyle (pioneer Arizona guide), Lewis Pyle, Zane Grey, George Haught (one of Babe's sons), Ben Copple, and Lee Doyle (Al's son).

Bear claw marks on an aspen tree.

Zane Grey on the rim, looking for bear.

Listening for the hounds.

George Takahashi, Grey's camp cook, with his first bear.

Zane and R.C.

A tired Zane Grey rests after a steep climb.

Zane Grey with wild turkeys.

Zane and R. C. Grey at camp in the Tonto Basin.

Babe Haught with quarry.

Zane Grey with Don Carlos, his favorite horse.

Zane Grey and his son, Romer, with bears.

Zane Grey with one of two bear cubs captured when their mother was killed. Grey preferred making pets out of bears to killing them, and in 1930, gave up hunting altogether and devoted his time to fishing.

Zane Grey and Lee Doyle with bears.

View after a sudden fall snowstorm.

Desolation: looking down over arid ridges to the stark Valley of Death.

Burros packed for the trip to Death Valley.

Grey tests the spines of a cholla cactus.

Desert graves.

The colorful Calico Mountains.

"Aw hullo!—I come down now," replied Takahashi.

I had seen both lynx and lion climb down out of a tree, but nothing except a squirrel could ever have beaten Takahashi. The spruce was fully one hundred and fifty feet high; and unless I made a great mistake the Jap descended in two minutes. He grinned from ear to ear.

"I no see you—no hear," he said. "You take me for big cat?"

"Yes, George, and I might have shot you. What were you doing up there?"

Takahashi brushed the needles and bark from his clothes. "I go out with little gun you give me. I hunt, no see squirrel. Go out no gun—see squirrel. I chase him up tree—I climb high—awful high. No good. Squirrel he too quick. He run right over me—get away."

Takahashi laughed with me. I believed he was laughing at what he considered the surprising agility of the squirrel, while I was laughing at him. Here was another manifestation of the Jap's simplicity and capacity. If all Japanese were like Takahashi they were a wonderful people. Men are men because they do things. The Persians were trained to sweat freely at least once every day of their lives. It seemed to me that if a man did not sweat every day, which was to say—labor hard—he very surely was degenerating physically. I could learn a great deal from George Takahashi. Right there I told him that my father had been a famous squirrel hunter in his day. He had such remarkable eyesight that he could espy the ear of a squirrel projecting above the highest limb of a tall white oak. And he was such a splendid shot that he had often "barked" squirrels, as was a noted practice of the old pioneer. I had to explain to Takahashi that this practice consisted of shooting a bullet to hit the bark right under the squirrel, and the concussion would so stun it that it would fall as if dead.

"Aw my goodnish—your daddy more better shot than you!" ejaculated Takahashi.

"Yes indeed he was," I replied, reflectively, as in a flash the long-past boyhood days recurred in memory. Hunting days—playing days of boyhood were the best of life. It seemed to me that one of the few reasons I still had for

clinging to hunting was this keen, thrilling hark back to early
days. Books first—then guns—then fishing poles—so ran the
list of material possessions dear to my heart as a lad.

That night was moonlight, cold, starry, with a silver sheen
on the spectral spruces. During the night there came a change;
it rained—first a drizzle, then a heavy downpour, and at
five-thirty a roar of hail on the tent. This music did not last
long. At seven o'clock the thermometer registered thirty-four
degrees, but there was no frost. The morning was somewhat
cloudy or foggy, with promise of clearing.

We took the hounds over to See Canyon, and while Edd
and Nielsen went down with them, the rest of us waited
above for developments. Scarcely had they more than time
enough to reach the gorge below when the pack burst into full
chorus. Haught led the way then around the rough rim for
better vantage points. I was mounted on one of the horses Lee
had gotten for me—a fine, spirited animal named Stockings.
Probably he had been a cavalry horse. He was a bay with
white feet, well built and powerful, though not over medium
size. One splendid feature about him was that a saddle appeared to fit him so snugly it never slipped. And another
feature, infinitely the most attractive to me, was his easy gait.
His trot and lope were so comfortable and swinging, like the
motion of a rocking-chair, that I could ride him all day with
pleasure. But when it came to chasing after hounds and bears
along the rim Stockings gave me trouble. Too eager, too
spirited, he would not give me time to choose the direction.
He jumped ditches and gullies, plunged into bad jumbles or
rock, tried to hurdle logs too high for him, carried me under
low branches and through dense thickets, and in general
showed he was exceedingly willing to chase after the pack,
but ignorant of rough forest travel. Owing to this I fell
behind, and got out of hearing of both hounds and men, and
eventually found myself lost somewhere on the west side of
See Canyon. To get out I had to turn my back to the sun,
travel west till I came to the rim above Horton Thicket, and
from there return to camp, arriving rather late in the afternoon.

All the men had returned, and all the hounds except Buck.
I was rather surprised and disturbed to find the Haughts in a

high state of dudgeon. Edd looked pale and angry. Upon
questioning Nielsen I learned that the hounds had at once
struck a fresh bear track in See Canyon. Nielsen and Edd had
not followed far before they heard a hound yelping in pain.
They found Buck caught in a bear trap. The rest of the
hounds came upon a little bear cub, caught in another trap,
and killed it. Nielsen said it had evidently been a prisoner for
some days, being very poor and emaciated. Fresh tracks of
the mother bear were proof that she had been around trying to
save it or minister to it. There were trappers in See Canyon
and between bear hunters and trappers manifestly there was
no love lost. Edd said they had as much right to trap as we
had to hunt, but that was not the question. There had been
opportunity to tell the Haughts about the big number four bear
traps set in See Canyon. But they did not tell it. Edd had
brought the dead cub back to our camp. It was a pretty little
bear cub, about six months old, with a soft silky brown coat.
No one had to look at it twice to see how it had suffered.

This matter of trapping wild animals is singularly hateful to
me. Bad enough is it to stalk deer to shoot them for their
meat, but at least this is a game where the deer have all the
advantage. Bad indeed it may be to chase bear with hounds,
but that is a hard, dangerous method of hunting which gives it
some semblance of fairness. Most of my bear hunts proved to
me that I ran more risks than the bears. To set traps, however, to hide big iron-springed, spike-toothed traps to catch
and clutch wild animals alive, and hold them till they died or
starved or gnawed off their feet, or until the trapper chose to
come with his gun or club to end the miserable business—
what indeed shall I call that? Cruel—base—cowardly!

It cannot be defended on moral grounds. But vast moneyed
interests are at stake. One of the greatest of American for-
tunes was built upon the brutal, merciless trapping of wild
animals for their furs. And in this fall of 1919 the prices of
fox, marten, beaver, raccoon, skunk, lynx, muskrat, mink,
otter, were higher by double than they had ever been. Trappers were going to reap a rich harvest. Well, everybody must
make a living; but is this trapping business honest, is it
manly? To my knowledge trappers are hardened. Market

fishermen are hardened, too, but the public eat fish. They do not eat furs. Now in cold climates and seasons furs are valuable to protect people who must battle with winter winds and sleet and ice; and against their use by such I daresay there is no justification for censure. But the vast number of furs go to deck the persons of vain women. I appreciate the beautiful contrast of fair skin against a background of sable fur, or silver fox, or rich, black, velvety seal. But beautiful women would be just as beautiful, just as warmly clothed in wool instead of fur. And infinitely better women! Not long ago I met a young woman in one of New York's fashionable hotels, and I remarked about the exquisite evening coat of fur she wore. She said she loved furs. She certainly was handsome, and she appeared to be refined, cultured, a girl of high class. And I said it was a pity women did not know or care where furs came from. She seemed surprised. Then I told her about the iron-jawed, spike-toothed traps hidden by the springs or on the runways of game—about the fox or beaver or marten seeking its food, training its young to fare for themselves— about the sudden terrible clutch of the trap, and then the frantic fear, the instinctive fury, the violent struggle—about the foot gnawed off by the beast that was too fierce to die a captive—about the hours of agony, the horrible thirst—the horrible days till death. And I concluded: "All because women are luxurious and vain!" She shuddered underneath the beautiful coat of furs, and seemed insulted.

Upon inquiry I learned from Nielsen that Buck was coming somewhere back along the trail hopping along on three legs. I rode on down to my camp, and procuring a bottle of iodine I walked back in the hope of doing Buck a good turn. During my absence he had reached camp, and was lying under an aspen, apart from the other hounds. Buck looked meaner and uglier and more distrustful than ever. Evidently this injury to his leg was a trick played upon him by his arch enemy man. I stood beside him, as he licked the swollen, bloody leg, and talked to him, as kindly as I knew how. And finally I sat down beside him. The trap-teeth had caught his right front leg just above the first joint, and from the position of the teeth marks and the way he moved his leg I had hopes that the bone was not broken. Apparently the big teeth had gone through on each side of the bone. When I tried gently to touch the swollen leg Buck growled ominously. He would have bitten me. I patted his head with one hand, and watching my chance, at length with the other I poured iodine over the open cuts. Then I kept patting him and holding his head until the iodine had become absorbed. Perhaps it was only my fancy, but it seemed that the ugly gleam in his distrustful eyes had become sheepish, as if he was ashamed of something he did not understand. That look more than ever determined me to try to find some way to his affections.

A camp-fire council that night resulted in plans to take a pack outfit, and ride west along the rim to a place Haught called Dude Creek. "Reckon we'll shore smoke up some bars along Dude," said Haught. "Never was in there but I jumped bars. Good deer an' turkey country, too."

Next day we rested the hounds, and got things into packing shape with the intention of starting early the following morning. But it rained on and off; and the day after that we could not find Haught's burros, and not until the fourth morning could we start. It turned out that Buck did not have a broken leg and had recovered surprisingly from the injury he had received. Aloof as he held himself it appeared certain he did not want to be left behind.

We rode all day along the old Crook road where the year before we had encountered so many obstacles. I remembered most of the road, but how strange it seemed to me, and what a proof of my mental condition on that memorable trip, that I did not remember all. Usually forest or desert ground I have traveled over I never forget. This ride, in the middle of October, when all the colors of autumn vied with the sunlight to make the forest a region of golden enchantment, was one of particular delight to me. I had begun to work and wear out the pain in my back. Every night I had suffered a little less and slept a little better, and every morning I had less and less of a struggle to get up and straighten out. Many a groan had I smothered. But now, when I got warmed up from riding or walking or sawing wood, the pain left me altogether and I forgot it. I had given myself heroic treatment, but my reward was in sight. My theory that the outdoor life would cure almost any ill of body or mind seemed to have earned another proof added to the long list.

At sunset we had covered about sixteen miles of rough road, and had arrived at a point where we were to turn away from the rim, down into a canyon named Barber Shop Canyon, where we were to camp.

Before turning aside I rode out to the rim for a look down at the section of country we were to hunt. What a pleasure to recognize the point from which Romer-boy had seen his first wild bear! It was a wonderful section of rim-rock country. I appeared to be at the extreme point of a vast ten-league promontory, rising high over the basin, where the rim was cut into canyons as thick as teeth of a saw. They were notched and v-shaped. Craggy russet-lichened cliffs, yellow and gold-stained rocks, old crumbling ruins of pinnacles crowned by pine thickets, ravines and gullies and canyons, choked with trees and brush all green-gold, purple-red, scarlet-fire—these indeed were the heights and depths, the wild, lonely ruggedness, the color and beauty of Arizona land. There were long, steep slopes of oak thickets, where the bears lived, long gray slides of weathered rocks, long slanting ridges of pine, descending for miles out and down into the green basin, yet always seeming to stand high above that rolling wilderness. The sun stood crossed by thin clouds—a golden blaze in a golden sky—sinking to meet a ragged horizon line of purple.

Here again was I confronted with the majesty and beauty of the earth, and with another and more striking effect of this vast tilted rim of mesa. I could see many miles to west and east. This rim was a huge wall of splintered rock, a colossal cliff, towering so high above the black basin below that ravines and canyons resembled ripples or dimples, darker lines of shade. And on the other side from its very edge, where the pine fringe began, it sloped gradually to the north, with heads of canyons opening almost at the crest. I saw one ravine begin its start not fifty feet from the rim.

Barber Shop Canyon had five heads, all running down like the fingers of a hand, to form the main canyon, which was deep, narrow, forested by giant pines. A round, level dell, watered by a murmuring brook, deep down among the many slopes, was our camp ground, and never had I seen one more desirable. The wind soughed in the lofty pine tops, but not a breeze reached down to this sheltered nook. With sunset gold on the high slopes our camp was shrouded in twilight shadows. R. C. and I stretched a canvas fly over a rope from tree to tree, staked down the ends, and left the sides open. Under this we unrolled our beds.

Night fell quickly down in that sequestered pit, and indeed it was black night. A blazing camp-fire enhanced the circling gloom, and invested the great brown pines with some weird aspect. The boys put up an old tent for the hounds. Poor Buck was driven out of this shelter by his canine rivals. I took pity upon him, and tied him at the foot of my bed. When R. C. and I crawled into our blankets we discovered Buck snugly settled between our beds, and wonderful to hear, he whined. "Well, Buck, old dog, you keep the skunks away," said R. C. And Buck emitted some kind of a queer sound, apparently meant to assure us that he would keep even a lion away. From my bed I could see the tips of the black pines close to the white stars. Before I dropped to sleep the night grew silent, except for the faint moan of wind and low murmur of brook.

We crawled out early, keen to run from the cold wash in the brook to the hot camp-fire. George and Edd had gone down the canyon after the horses, which had been hobbled and turned loose. Lee had remained with his father at Beaver Dam camp. For breakfast Takahashi had venison, biscuits, griddle cakes with maple syrup, and hot cocoa. I certainly did not begin on an empty stomach what augured to be a hard day. Buck hung around me this morning, and I subdued my generous impulses long enough to be convinced that he had undergone a subtle change. Then I fed him. Old Dan and Old Tom were witnesses of this procedure, which they regarded with extreme disfavor. And the pups tried to pick a fight with Buck.

By eight o'clock we were riding up the colored slopes, through the still forest, with the sweet, fragrant, frosty air nipping at our noses. A mile from camp we reached a notch

in the rim that led down to Dude Creek, and here Edd and
Nielsen descended with the hounds. The rest of us rode out to
a point there to await developments. The sun had already
flooded the basin with golden light; the east slopes of canyon
and rim were dark in shade. I sat on a mat of pine needles
near the rim, and looked, and cared not for passage of time.

But I was not permitted to be left to sensorial dreams.
Right under us the hounds opened up, filling the canyon full
of bellowing echoes. They worked down. Slopes below us
narrowed to promontories and along these we kept our gaze.
Suddenly Haught gave a jump, and rose, thumping to his
horse. "Saw a bar," he yelled. "Just got a glimpse of him
crossin' an open ridge. Come on." We mounted and chased
Haught over the roughest kind of rocky ground, to overtake
him at the next point on the rim. "Ride along, you fellars,"
he said, "an' each pick out a stand. Keep ahead of the dogs
an' look sharp."

Then it was in short order that I found myself alone,
Copple, R. C. and George Haught having got ahead of me. I
kept to the rim. The hounds could be heard plainly and also
the encouraging yells of Nielsen and Edd. Apparently the
chase was working along under me, in the direction I was
going. The baying of the pack, the scent of pine, the ring of
iron-shod hoofs on stone, the sense of wild, broken, vast
country, the golden void beneath and the purple-ranged
horizon—all these brought vividly and thrillingly to mind my
hunting days with Buffalo Jones along the north rim of the
Grand Canyon. I felt a pang, both for the past, and for my
friend and teacher, this last of the old plainsmen who had
died recently. In his last letter to me, written with a death-
stricken hand, he had talked of another hunt, of more adventure, of his cherished hope to possess an island in the north
Pacific, there to propagate wild animals—he had dreamed
again the dream that could never come true. I was riding with
my face to the keen, sweet winds of the wild, and he was
gone. No joy in life is ever perfect. I wondered if any grief
was ever wholly hopeless.

I came at length to a section of rim where huge timbered
steps reached out and down. Dismounting I tied Stockings,

and descended to the craggy points below, where I clambered
here and there, looking, listening. No longer could I locate
the hounds; now the baying sounded clear and sharp, close at
hand, and then hollow and faint, and far away. I crawled
under gnarled cedars, over jumbles of rock, around leaning
crags, until I got out to a point where I had such command of
slopes and capes, where the scene was so grand that I was
both thrilled and awed. Somewhere below me to my left were
the hounds still baying. The lower reaches of the rim consisted of ridges and gorges, benches and ravines, canyons and
promontories—a country so wild and broken that it seemed
impossible for hounds to travel it, let alone men. Above me,
to my right, stuck out a yellow point of rim, and beyond that
I knew there jutted out another point, and more and more
points on toward the west. George was yelling from one of
them, and I thought I heard a faint reply from R. C. or
Copple. I believed for the present they were too far westward
along the rim, and so I devoted my attention to the slopes
under me toward my left. But once my gaze wandered around,
and suddenly I espied a shiny black object moving along a
bare slope, far below. A bear! So thrilled and excited was I
that I did not wonder why this bear walked along so leisurely
and calmly. Assuredly he had not even heard the hounds. I
began to shoot, and in five rapid shots I spattered dust all
over him. Not until I had two more shots, one of which struck
close, did he begin to run. Then he got out of my sight. I
yelled and yelled to those ahead of me along the rim. Somebody answered, and next somebody began to shoot. How I
climbed and crawled and scuffled to get back to my horse!
Stockings answered to the spirit of the occasion. Like a deer
he ran around the rough rim, and I had to perform with the
agility of a contortionist to avoid dead snags of trees and
green branches. When I got to the point from which I had
calculated George had done his shooting I found no one. My
yells brought no answers. But I heard a horse cracking the
rocks behind me. Then up from far below rang the sharp
spangs of rifles in quick action. Nielsen and Edd were shooting. I counted seven shots. How the echoes rang from wall to
wall, to die hollow and faint in the deep canyons!

I galloped ahead to the next point, finding only the tracks of R. C.'s boots. Everywhere I peered for the bear I had sighted, and at intervals I yelled. For all the answer I got I might as well have been alone on the windy rim of the world. My voice seemed lost in immensity. Then I rode westward, then back eastward, and to and fro until both Stockings and I were weary. At last I gave up, and took a good, long rest under a pine on the rim. Not a shot, not a yell, not a sound but wind and the squall of a jay disrupted the peace of that hour. I profited by this lull in the excitement by more means than one, particularly in sight of a flock of wild pigeons. They alighted in the tops of pines below me, so that I could study them through my field glass. They were considerably larger than doves, dull purple color on the back, light on the breast, with ringed or barred neck. Haught had assured me that birds of this description were indeed the famous wild pigeons, now almost extinct in the United States. I remembered my father telling me he had seen flocks that darkened the skies. These pigeons appeared to have swift flight.

Another feature of this rest along the rim was a sight just as beautiful as that of the pigeons, though not so rare; and it was the flying of clouds of colored autumn leaves on the wind.

The westering of the sun advised me that the hours had fled, and it was high time for me to bestir myself toward camp. On my way back I found Haught, his son George, Copple and R. C. waiting for Edd and Nielsen to come up over the rim, and for me to return. They asked for my story. Then I learned theirs. Haught had kept even with the hounds, but had seen only the brown bear that had crossed the ridge early in the day. Copple had worked far westward, to no avail. R. C. had been close to George and me, had heard our bullets pat, yet had been unable to locate any bear. To my surprise it turned out that George had shot at a brown bear when I had supposed it was my black one. Whereupon Haught said: "Reckon Edd an' Nielsen smoked up some other bear."

One by one the hounds climbed over the rim and wearily lay down beside us. Down the long, grassy, cedared aisle I saw Edd and Nielsen plodding up. At length they reached us wet and dusty and thirsty. When Edd got his breath he said:

"Right off we struck a hot trail. Bear with eleven-inch track. He'd come down to drink last night. Hounds worked up thet yeller oak thicket, an' somewhere Sue an' Rock jumped him out of his bed. He run down, an' he made some racket. Took to the low slopes an' hit up lively all the way down Dude, then crossed, climbed around under thet bare point of rock. Here some of the hounds caught up with him. We heard a pup yelp, an' after a while Kaiser Bill come sneakin' back. It was awful thick down in the canyon so we climbed the east side high enough to see. An' we were workin' down when the pack bayed the bear round thet bare point. It was up an' across from us. Nielsen an' I climbed on a rock. There was an open rock-slide where we thought the bear would show. It was five hundred yards. We ought to have gone across an' got a stand higher up. Well, pretty soon we saw him come paddlin' out of the brush—a big grizzly, almost black, with a frosty back. He was a silvertip all right. Niels an' I began to shoot. An' thet bear began to hump himself. He was mad, too. His fur stood up like a ruffle on his neck. Niels got four shots an' I got three. Reckon one of us stung him a little. Lordy, how he run! An' his last jump off the slide was a header into the brush. He crossed the canyon, an' climbed thet high east slope of Dude, goin' over the pass where father killed the big cinnamon three years ago. The hounds stuck to his trail. It took us an hour or more to climb up to thet pass. Broad bear trail goes over. We heard the hounds 'way down in the canyon on the other side. Niels an' I worked along the ridge, down an' around, an' back to Dude Creek. I kept callin' the hounds till they all came back. They couldn't catch him. He sure was a jack-rabbit for runnin'. Reckon thet's all. . . . Now who was smokin' shells up on the rim?''

When all was told and talked over Haught said: "Wal, you can just bet we put up two brown bears an' one black bear, an' thet old Jasper of a silvertip.''

How hungry and thirsty and tired I was when we got back to camp! The day had been singularly rich in exciting thrills and sensorial perceptions. I called to the Jap: "I'm starv-ved to death!'' And Takahashi, who had many times heard my little boy Loren yell that, grinned all over his dusky face. "Aw, lots good things pretty soon!''

After supper we lounged around a cheerful, crackling camp-fire. The blaze roared in the breeze, the red embers glowed white and opal, the smoke swooped down and curled away into the night shadows. Old Dan, as usual, tried to sit in the fire, and had to be rescued. Buck came to me where I sat with my back to a pine, my feet to the warmth. He was lame to-night, having run all day on that injured leg. The other dogs lay scattered around in range of the heat. Natural indeed was it then, in such an environment, after talking over the auspicious start of our hunt at Dude Creek, that we should drift to the telling of stories.

Sensing this drift I opened the hour of reminiscence and told some of my experiences in the jungle of southern Mexico. Copple immediately topped my stories by more wonderful and hair-raising ones about his own adventures in northern Mexico. These stirred Nielsen to talk about the Seri Indians, and their cannibalistic traits; and from these he drifted to the Yuma Indians. Speaking of their remarkable stature and strength he finally got to the subject of giants of brawn and bone in Norway.

One young Norwegian was eight feet tall and broad in proportion. His employer was a captain of a fishing boat. One time, on the way to their home port, a quarrel arose about money due the young giant, and in his anger he heaved the anchor overboard. That of course halted the boat, and it stayed halted, because the captain and crew could not heave the heavy anchor without the help of their brawny comrade. Finally the money matter was adjusted, and the young giant heaved the anchor without assistance. Nielsen went on to tell that this fisherman of such mighty frame had a beautiful young wife whom he adored. She was not by any means a small or frail girl—rather the contrary—but she appeared diminutive beside her giant husband. One day he returned from a long absence on the sea. When his wife, in her joy, ran into his arms, he gave her such a tremendous hug that he crushed her chest, and she died. In his grief the young husband went insane and did not survive her long.

Next Nielsen told a story about Norwegians sailing to the Arctic on a scientific expedition. Just before the long polar night of darkness set in there arose a necessity for the ship and crew to return to Norway. Two men must be left in the Arctic to care for the supplies until the ship came back. The captain called for volunteers. There were two young men in the crew, and from childhood they had been playmates, school-mates, closer than brothers, and inseparable even in man-hood. One of these young men said to his friend: "I'll stay if you will." And the other quickly agreed. After the ship sailed, and the land of the midnight sun had become icy and black, one of these comrades fell ill, and soon died. The living one placed the body in the room with the ship supplies, where it froze stiff; and during all the long polar night of solitude and ghastly gloom he lived next to this sepulchre that contained his dead friend. When the ship returned the crew found the living comrade an old man with hair as white as snow, and never in his life afterward was he seen to smile.

These stories stirred my emotions like Doyle's tale about Jones' Ranch. How wonderful, beautiful, terrible and tragical is human life! Again I heard the still, sad music of humanity, the eternal beat and moan of the waves upon a lonely shingle shore. Who would not be a teller of tales?

Copple followed Nielsen with a story about a prodigious feat of his own—a story of incredible strength and endurance, which at first I took to be a satire on Nielsen's remarkable narrative. But Copple seemed deadly serious, and I began to see that he possessed a strange simplicity of exaggeration. The boys thought Copple stretched the truth a little, but I thought that he believed what he told.

Haught was a great teller of tales, and his first story of the evening happened to be about his brother Bill. They had a long chase after a bear and became separated. Bill was new at the game, and he was a peculiar fellow anyhow. Much given to talking to himself! Haught finally rode to the edge of a ridge and espied Bill under a pine in which the hounds had treed a bear. Bill did not hear Haught's approach, and on the moment he was stalking round the pine, swearing at the bear, which clung to a branch about half way up. Then Haught discovered two more full-grown bears up in the top of the pine, the presence of which Bill had not the remotest suspicion. "Ahuh! you ole black Jasper!" Bill was yelling. "I treed you an' in a minnit I'm agoin' to assassinate you. Chased me about a hundred miles——! An' thought you'd fool me, didn't you? Why, I've treed more bears than you ever saw——! You needn't look at me like thet, 'cause I'm mad as a hornet. I'm agoin' to assassinate you in a minnit an' skin your black har off, I am——"

"Bill," interrupted Haught, "what are you goin' to do about the other two bears up in the top of the tree?"

Bill was amazed to hear and see his brother, and greatly astounded and tremendously elated to discover the other two bears. He yelled and acted as one demented. "Three black Jaspers! I've treed you all. An' I'm agoin' to assassinate you all!"

"See here, Bill," said Haught, "before you begin that assassinatin' make up your mind not to cripple any of them. You've got to shoot straight, so they'll be dead when they fall. If they're only crippled, they'll kill the hounds."

Bill was insulted at any suggestions as to his possible poor marksmanship. But this happened to be his first experience with bears in trees. He began to shoot and it took nine shots for him to dislodge the bears. Worse than that they all tumbled out of the tree—apparently unhurt. The hounds, of course, attacked them, and there arose a terrible uproar. Haught had to run down to save his dogs. Bill was going to shoot right into the melee, but Haught knocked the rifle up, and forbid him to use it. Then Bill ran into the thick of the fray to beat off the hounds. Haught became exceedingly busy himself, and finally disposed of two of the bears. Then hearing angry bawls and terrific yells he turned to see Bill climbing a tree with a big black bear tearing the seat out of his pants. Haught disposed of this bear also. Then he said: "Bill, I thought you was goin' to assassinate them." Bill slid down out of the tree, very pale and disheveled. "By Golly, I'll skin 'em anyhow!"

Haught had another brother named Henry, who had come to Arizona from Texas, and had brought a half-hound with him. Henry offered to wager this dog was the best bear chaser in the country. The general impression Henry's hound gave was that he would not chase a rabbit. Finally Haught took his brother Henry and some other men on a bear hunt. There were wagers made as to the quality of Henry's half-hound. When at last Haught's pack struck a hot scent, and were off with the men riding fast behind, Henry's half-breed loped alongside his master, paying no attention to the wild baying of the pack. He would look up at Henry as if to say: "No hurry, boss. Wait a little. Then I'll show them!" He loped along, wagging his tail, evidently enjoying this race with his master. After a while the chase grew hotter. Then Henry's half-hound ran ahead a little way, and came back to look up wisely, as if to say: "Not time yet!" After a while, when the chase grew very hot indeed, Henry's wonderful canine let out a wild yelp, darted ahead, overtook the pack and took the lead in the chase, literally chewing the heels of the bear till he treed. Haught and his friends lost all the wagers

The most remarkable bears in this part of Arizona were what Haught called blue bears, possibly some kind of a cross between brown and black. This species was a long, slim, blue-furred bear with unusually large teeth and very long claws. So different from ordinary bears that it appeared another species. The blue bear could run like a greyhound, and keep it up all day and all night. Its power of endurance was incredible. In Haught's twenty years of hunting there he had seen a number of blue bears and had killed two. Haught chased one all day with young and fast hounds. He went to camp, but the hounds stuck to the chase. Next day Haught followed the hounds and bear from Dude Creek over into Verde Canyon, back to Dude Creek, and then back to Verde again. Here Haught gave out, and was on his way home when he met the blue bear padding along as lively as ever.

I never tired of listening to Haught. He had killed over a hundred bears, many of them vicious grizzlies, and he had often escaped by a breadth of a hair, but the killing stories were not the most interesting to me. Haught had lived a singularly elemental life. He never knew what to tell me, because I did not know what to ask for, so I just waited for stories, experiences, woodcraft, natural history and the like, to come when they would. Once he had owned an old bay horse named Moze. Under any conditions of weather or country Moze could find his way back to camp. Haught would let go the bridle, and Moze would stick up his ears, look about him, and circle home. No matter if camp had been just where Haught had last thrown a packsaddle!

When Haught first came to Arizona and began his hunting up over the rim he used to get down in the cedar country, close to the desert. Here he heard of a pure black antelope that was the leader of a herd of ordinary color, which was a grayish white. The day came when Haught saw this black antelope. It was a very large, beautiful stag, the most noble and wild and sagacious animal Haught had ever seen. For years he tried to stalk it and kill it, and so did other hunters. But no hunter ever got even a shot at it. Finally this black antelope disappeared and was never heard of again.

By this time Copple had been permitted a long breathing spell, and now began a tale calculated to outdo the Arabian Nights. I envied his most remarkable imagination. His story had to do with hunting meat for a mining camp in Mexico. He got so expert with a rifle that he never aimed at deer. Just threw his gun, as was a habit of gun-fighters! Once the camp was out of meat, and also he was out of ammunition. Only one shell left! He came upon a herd of deer licking salt at a deer lick. They were small deer and he wanted several or all of them. So he manoeuvred around and waited until five of the deer had lined up close together. Then, to make sure, he aimed so as to send his one bullet through their necks. Killed the whole five in one shot!

We were all reduced to a state of mute helplessness and completely at Copple's mercy. Next he gave us one of his animal tales. He was hunting along the gulf shore on the coast of Sonora, where big turtles come out to bask in the sun and big jaguars come down to prowl for meat. One morning he saw a jaguar jump on the back of a huge turtle, and begin to paw at its neck. Promptly the turtle drew in head and flippers, and was safe under its shell. The jaguar scratched and clawed at a great rate, but to no avail. Then the big cat turned round and seized the tail of the turtle and began to chew it. Where- upon the turtle stuck out its head, opened its huge mouth and grasped the tail of the jaguar. First to give in was the cat. He let go and let out a squall. But the turtle started to crawl off, got going strong, and dragged the jaguar into the sea and drowned him. With naive earnestness Copple assured his mute listeners that he could show them the exact spot in Sonora where this happened.

Retribution inevitably overtakes transgressors. Copple in his immense loquaciousness was not transgressing much, for he really was no greater dreamer than I, but the way he put things made us want to see the mighty hunter have a fall.

We rested the hounds next day, and I was glad to rest myself. About sunset Copple rode up to the rim to look for his mules. We all heard him shoot eight times with his rifle and two with his revolver. Everybody said: "Turkeys! Ten turkeys—maybe a dozen, if Copple got two in line!" And we were all glad to think so. We watched eagerly for him, but he did not return till dark. He seemed vstly sore at himself. What a remarkable hard luck story he told! He had come upon a flock of turkeys, and they were rather difficult to see. All of them were close, and running fast. He shot eight times at eight turkeys and missed them all. Too dark—brush—trees— running like deer. Copple had a dozen excuses. Then he saw a turkey on a log ten feet away. He shot twice. The turkey was a knot, and he had missed even that.

Thereupon I seized my opportunity and reminded all present how Copple had called out: "Turkey number one! Turkey number two!" the day I had missed so many. Then I said:

"Ben, you must have yelled out to-night like this." And I raised my voice high.

"Turkey number one—Nix! . . . Turkey number two— missed, by Gosh! . . . Turkey number three—never touched him! . . . Turkey number four—*No!* . . . Turkey number five—*Aw, I'm shootin' blank shells!* . . . Turkey number six on the log—BY THUNDER, I CAN'T SEE STRAIGHT!"

We all had our fun at Copple's expense. The old bear hunter, Haught, rolled on the ground, over and over, and roared in his mirth.

VII

Early next morning before the sun had tipped the pines with gold I went down Barber Shop Canyon with Copple to look for our horses. During the night our stock had been chased by a lion. We had all been awakened by their snorting and stampeding. We found our horses scattered, the burros gone, and Copple's mules still squared on guard, ready to fight. Copple assured me that this formation of his mules on guard was an infallible sign of lions prowling around. One of these mules he had owned for ten years and it was indeed the most intelligent beast I ever saw in the woods.

We found three beaver dams across the brook, one about fifty feet long, and another fully two hundred. Fresh turkey tracks showed in places, and on the top of the longer dam, fresh made in the mud, were lion tracks as large as the crown of my hat. How sight of them made me tingle all over! Here was absolute proof of the prowling of one of the great cats.

Beaver tracks were everywhere. They were rather singular looking tracks, the front feet being five-toed, and the back three-toed, and webbed. Near the slides on the bank the water was muddy, showing that the beaver had been at work early. These animals worked mostly at night, but sometimes at sunset and sunrise. They were indeed very cautious and wary. These dams had just been completed and no aspens had yet been cut for food. Beaver usually have two holes to their home, one under the water, and the other out on the bank. We found one of these outside burrows and it was nearly a foot wide.

Upon our return to camp with the horses Haught said he could put up that lion for us, and from the size of its track he judged it to be a big one. I did not want to hunt lions and R. C. preferred to keep after bears. "Wal," said Haught, "I'll take an off day an' chase thet lion. Had a burro killed here a couple of years ago."

So we rode out with the hounds on another bear hunt. Pyle's Canyon lay to the east of Dude Creek, and we decided to run it that day. Edd and Nielsen started down with the hounds. Copple and I followed shortly afterward with the intention of descending mid-way, and then working along the ridge crests and promontories. The other boys remained on the rim to take up various stands as occasion called for.

I had never been on as steep slopes as these under the rim. They were grassy, brushy, rocky, but it was their steepness that made them so hard to travel. Right off, half way down, we started a herd of bucks. The noise they made sounded like cattle. We found tracks of half a dozen. "Lots of deer under the rim," declared Copple, his eyes gleaming. "They're feedin' on acorns. Here's where you'll get your big buck." After that I kept a sharp lookout, arguing with myself that a buck close at hand was worth a lot of bears down in the brush.

Presently we changed a direct descent to work gradually along the slopes toward a great level bench covered with pines. We had to cross gravel patches and pits where avalanches had slid, and at last, gaining the bench we went through the pine grove, out to a manzanita thicket, to a rocky point where the ledges were toppling and dangerous. The stand here afforded a magnificent view. We were now down in the thick of this sloped and canyoned and timbered wildness; no longer above it, and aloof from it. The dry smell of pine filled the air. When we finally halted to listen we at once heard the baying of the hounds in the black notch below us. We watched and listened. And presently across open patches we saw the flash of deer, and then Rock and Buck following them. Thus were my suspicions of Rock fully confirmed. Copple yelled down to Edd that some of the hounds were running deer, but apparently Edd was too far away to hear.

Still, after a while we heard the mellow tones of Edd's horn, calling in the hounds. And then he blew the signal to acquaint all of us above that he was going down around the point to drive the next canyon. Copple and I had to choose between climbing back to the rim or trying to cross the slopes and head the gorges, and ascend the huge ridge that separated Pyle's Canyon from the next canyon. I left the question to Copple, with the result that we stayed below.

We were still high up, though when we gazed aloft at the rim we felt so far down, and the slopes were steep, stony, soft in places and slippery in others, with deep cuts and patches of manzanita. No stranger was I to this beautiful treacherous Spanish brush! I shared with Copple a dislike of it almost equal to that inspired by cactus. We soon were hot, dusty, dry, and had begun to sweat. The immense distances of the place were what continually struck me. Distances that were deceptive—that looked short and were interminable! That was Arizona. We covered miles in our detours and we had to travel fast because we knew Edd could round the base of the lower points in quick time.

Above the head of the third gorge Copple and I ran across an enormous bear track, fresh in the dust, leading along an old bear trail. This track measured twelve inches. "He's an old Jasper, as Haught says," declared Copple. "Grizzly. An' you can bet he heard the dogs an 'got movin' away from here. But he ain't scared. He was walkin'."

I forgot the arduous toil. How tight and cool and prickling the feel of my skin! The fresh track of a big grizzly would rouse the hunter in any man. We made sure how fresh this track was by observing twigs and sprigs of manzanita just broken. The wood was green, and wet with sap. Old Bruin had not escaped our eyes any too soon. We followed this bear trail, evidently one used for years. It made climbing easy for us. Trust a big, heavy, old grizzly to pick out the best traveling over rough country! This fellow, I concluded, had the eye of a surveyor. His trail led gradually toward a wonderful crag-crowned ridge that rolled and heaved down from the rim. It had a dip or saddle in the middle, and rose from that to the lofty mesa, and then on the lower side, rose to a bare, round point of gray rock, a landmark, a dome-shaped tower where the gods of that wild region might have kept their vigil.

Long indeed did it take us to climb up the bear trail to where it crossed the saddle and went down on the other side into a canyon so deep and wild that it was purple. This saddle was really a remarkable place—a natural trail and outlet and escape for bears traveling from one canyon to another. Our bear tracks showed fresh, and we saw where they led down a steep, long, dark aisle between pines and spruces to a dense black thicket below. The saddle was about twenty feet wide, and on each side of it rose steep rocks, affording most effective stands for a hunter to wait and watch.

We rested then, and listened. There was only a little wind, and often it fooled us. It sounded like the baying of hounds, and now like the hallooing of men, and then like the distant peal of a horn. By and bye Copple said he heard the hounds. I could not be sure. Soon we indeed heard the deep-sounding, wild bay of Old Dan, the course, sharp, ringing bay of Old Tom, and then, less clear, the chorus from the other hounds. Edd had started them on a trail up this magnificent canyon at our feet. After a while we heard Edd's yell, far away, but clear: "Hi! Hi!" We could see a part of the thicket, shaggy and red and gold; and a mile or more of the opposite wall of the canyon. No rougher, wilder place could have been imagined than this steep slope of bluffs, ledges, benches, all matted with brush, and spotted with pines. Holes and caves and cracks showed, and yellow blank walls, and bronze points, and green slopes, and weathered slides.

Soon the baying of the hounds appeared to pass below and beyond us, up the canyon to our right, a circumstance that worried Copple. "Let's go farther up," he kept saying. But I was loath to leave that splendid stand. The baying of the hounds appeared to swing round closer under us; to ring, to swell, to thicken until it was a continuous and melodious, wild, echoing roar. The narrowing walls of the canyon threw the echoes back and forth.

Presently I espied moving dots, one blue, one brown, on the opposite slope. they were Haught and his son Edd slowly and laboriously climbing up the steep bluff. How like snails they climbed! Theirs was indeed a task. A yell pealed out now and then, and though it seemed to come from an entirely different direction it surely must have come from the Haughts. Presently some one high on the rim answered with like yells. The chase was growing hotter.

"They've got a bear up somewhere," cried Copple, excitedly. And I agreed with him.

Then we were startled by the sharp crack of a rifle from the rim.

"The ball's open! Get your pardners, boys," exclaimed Copple, with animation.

"Ben, wasn't that a .30 Gov't?" I asked.

"Sure was," he replied. "Must have been R. C. openin' up. Now look sharp!"

I gazed everywhere, growing more excited and thrilled. Another shot from above, farther off and from a different rifle, augmented our stirring expectation.

Copple left our stand and ran up over the ridge, and then down under and along the base of a rock wall. I had all I could do to keep up with him. We got perhaps a hundred yards when we heard the spang of Haught's .30 Gov't. Following this his big, hoarse voice bawled out: "He's goin' to the left—to the left!" That sent us right about face, to climbing, scrambling, running and plunging back to our first stand at the saddle, where we arrived breathless and eager.

Edd was climbing higher up, evidently to reach the level top of the bluff above, and Haught was working farther up the canyon, climbing a little. Copple yelled with all his might: "Where's the bear?"

"Bar everywhar!" pealed back Haught's stentorian voice. How the echoes clapped!

Just then Copple electrified me with a wild shout. *"Wehow! I see him. . . . What a whopper!"* He threw up his rifle: *spang—spang—spang—spang—spang*.

His aim was across the canyon. I heard his bullets strike. I strained my eyes in flashing gaze everywhere. "Where? Where?" I cried, wildly.

"There!" shouted Copple, keenly, and he pointed across the canyon. "He's goin' over the bench—above Edd. . . . Now he's out of sight. Watch just over Edd. He'll cross that bench, go round the head of the little canyon, an' come out on the other side, under the bare bluff. . . . Watch sharp—right by that big spruce with the dead top. . . . He's a grizzly an' as big as a horse."

I looked until my eyes hurt. All I said was: "Ben, you saw game first to-day." Suddenly a large, dark brown object, furry and grizzled, huge and round, moved out of the shadow under the spruce and turned to go along the edge in the open sunlight.

"Oh! look at him!" I yelled. A strong, hot gust of blood ran all over me and I thrilled till I shook. When I aimed at the bear I could see him through the circle of my peep sight, but when I moved the bead of the front sight upon him it almost covered him up. The distance was far—more than a thousand yards—over half a mile—we calculated afterward. But I tried to draw a bead on the big, wagging brown shape and fired till my rifle was empty.

Meanwhile Copple had reloaded. "You watch while I shoot," he said. "Tell me where I'm hittin'."

Wonderful was it to see how swiftly he could aim and shoot. I saw a puff of dust. "Low, Ben!" Spang rang his rifle. "High!" Again he shot, wide this time. He emptied his magazine. "Smoke him now!" he shouted, gleefully. "I'll watch while you shoot."

"It's too far, Ben," I replied, as I jammed the last shell in the receiver.

"No—no. It's only we don't hold right. Aim a little coarse," said Copple. "Gee, ain't he some bear! 'No scared tall,' as the Jap says. . . . He's one of the old sheep-killers. He'll weigh half a ton. Smoke him now!"

My excitement was intense. It seemed, however, I was most consumed with admiration for that grizzly. Not in the least was he afraid. He walked along the rough places, trotted along the ledges, and here and there he halted to gaze below him. I waited for one of these halts, aimed a trifle high, and fired. The grizzly made a quick, angry movement and then jumped up on a ledge. He jumped like a rabbit.

"You hit close that time," yelled Ben. "Hold the same way—a little coarser."

My next bullet struck a puff from rock above the bear, and my third, hitting just in front of him, as he was on a yellow ledge, covered him with dust. He reared, and wheeling, sheered back and down the step he had mounted, and disappeared in a clump of brush. I shot into that. We heard my bullet crack the twigs. But it routed him out, and then my last shot hit far under him.

Copple circled his mouth with his hands and bellowed to the Haughts: "Climb! Climb! Hurry! Hurry! He's just above you—under that bluff."

The Haughts heard, and evidently tried to do all in their power, but they moved like snails. Then Copple fired five more shots, quick, yet deliberate, and he got through before I had reloaded; and as I began my third magazine Copple was so swift in reloading that his first shot mingled with my second. How we made the welkin ring! Wild yells pealed down from the rim. Somewhere from the purple depths below Nielsen's giant's voice rolled up. The Haughts opposite answered with their deep, hoarse yells. Old Dan and Old Tom bayed like distant thunder. The young hounds let out a string of sharp, keen yelps. Copple added his Indian cry, high-pitched and wild, to the pandemonium. But I could not shoot and screech at one and the same time.

"Hurry, Ben," I said, as I finished my third set of five shots, the last shot of which was my best and knocked dirt in the face of the grizzly.

Again he reared. This time he appeared to locate our direction. Above the bedlam of yells and bays and yelps and echoes I imagined I heard the grizzly roar. He was now getting farther along the base of the bluff, and I saw that he would escape us. My rifle barrel was hot as fire. My fingers were all thumbs. I jammed a shell into the receiver. My last chance had fled! But Copple's big, brown, swift hands fed shells to his magazine as ears of corn go to a grinder. He had a way of poking the base of a shell straight down into the receiver and making it snap forward and down. Then he fired five more shots as swiftly as he had reloaded. Some of these hit close to our quarry. The old grizzly slowed up, and looked across, and wagged his huge head.

"My gun's on fire all right," said Copple, grimly, as he loaded still more rapidly. Carefully he aimed and pulled trigger. The grizzly gave a spasmodic jerk as if stung and suddenly he made a prodigious leap off a ledge, down into a patch of brush, where he threshed like a lassoed elephant.

"Ben, you hit him!" I yelled, excitedly.

"Only made him mad. He's not hurt. . . . See, he's up again. . . . Will you look at that!"

The grizzly appeared to roll out of the brush, and like a huge furry ball of brown, he bounced down the thicketed slope to an open slide where he unrolled, and stretched into a run. Copple got two more shots before he was out of sight.

"Gone!" ejaculated Copple. "An' we never fetched him! . . . He ain't hurt. Did you see him pile down an' roll off that slope? . . . Let's see. I got twenty-three shots at him. How many had you?"

"I had fifteen."

"Say, it was some fun, wasn't it—smokin' him along there? But we ought to have fetched the old sheepkiller. . . . Wonder what's happened to the other fellows."

We looked about us. Not improbably the exciting moments had been few in number, yet they seemed long indeed. The Haughts had gotten to the top of the bluff, and were tearing through the brush toward the point Copple had designated. They reached it too late.

"Where is he?" yelled Edd.

"Gone!" boomed Copple. "Runnin' down the canyon. Call the dogs an' go down after him."

When the Haughts came out into the open upon that bench one of the pups and the spotted hound, Rock, were with them. Old Dan and Old Tom were baying up at the head of the canyon, and Sue could be heard yelping somewhere else. Bear trails seemingly were abundant near our whereabouts. Presently the Haughts disappeared at the back of the bench where the old grizzly had gone down, and evidently they put the two hounds on his trail.

"That grizzly will climb over round the lower end of this ridge," declared Copple. "We want to be there."

So we hurriedly left our stand, and taking to the south side of the ridge, we ran and walked and climbed and plunged down along the slope. Keeping up with Copple on foot was harder than riding after Edd and George. When soon we reached a manzanita thicket I could no longer keep Copple in sight. He was so powerful that he just crashed through, but I had to worm my way, and walk over the tops of the bushes, like a tight-rope performer. Of all strong, thick, spiky brush manzanita was the worst.

In half an hour I joined Copple at the point under the dome-topped end of the ridge, only to hear the hounds apparently working back up the canyon. There was nothing for us to do but return to our stand at the saddle. Copple hurried faster than ever. But I had begun to tire and I could not keep up with him. But as I had no wild cravings to meet that old grizzly face to face all by myself in a manzanita thicket I did manage by desperate efforts to keep the Indian in sight. When I reached our stand I was wet and exhausted. After the hot, stifling, dusty glare of the yellow slope and the burning of the manzanita brush, the cool shade was a welcome change.

Somewhere all the hounds were baying. Not for some time could we locate the Haughts. Finally with the aid of my glass we discovered them perched high upon the bluff above where our grizzly had gone round. It appeared that Edd was pointing across the canyon and his father was manifesting a keen interest. We did not need the glass then to tell that they saw a bear. Both leveled their rifles and fired, apparently across the canyon. Then they stood like statues.

"I'll go down into the thicket," said Copple. "Maybe I can get a shot. An' anyway I want to see our grizzly's tracks." With that he started down, and once on the steep bear trail he slid rather than walked, and soon was out of my sight. After that I heard him crashing through thicket and brush. Soon this sound ceased. The hounds, too, had quit baying and the wind had lulled. Not a rustle of a leaf! All the hunters were likewise silent. I enjoyed a lonely hour there watching and listening, not however without apprehensions of a bear coming along. Certain I was that this canyon, which I christened Bear Canyon, had been full of bears.

At length I espied Copple down on the edge of the opposite slope. The way he toiled along proved how rough was the going. I watched him through my glasses, and was again impressed with the strange difference between the semblance of distance and the reality. Every few steps Copple would halt to rest. He had to hold on to the brush and in the bare places where he could not reach a bush he had to dig his heels into the earth to keep from sliding down. In time he ascended to the place where our grizzly had rolled down, and from there he yelled up to the Haughts, high above him. They answered, and soon disappeared on the far side of the bluff. Copple also

disappeared going round under the wall of yellow rock. Perhaps in fifteen minutes I heard them yell, and then a wild
clamor of the hounds. Some of the pack had been put on the
trail of our grizzly; but gradually the sound grew farther
away.

This was too much for me. I decided to go down into the
canyon. Forthwith I started. It was easy to go down! As a
matter of fact it was hard not to slide down like a streak. That
long, dark, narrow aisle between the spruces had no charm
for me anyway. Suppose I should meet a bear coming up as I
was sliding down! I sheered off and left the trail, and also
Copple's tracks. This was a blunder. I came out into more
open slope, but steeper, and harder to cling on. Ledges
cropped out, cliffs and ravines obstructed my passage and
trees were not close enough to help me much. Some long
slopes of dark, mossy, bare earth I actually ran down, trusting
to light swift steps rather than slow careful ones. It was
exhilarating, that descent under the shady spruces. The lower
down I got the smaller and more numerous the trees. I could
see where they left off to the dense thicket that choked the
lower part of the v-shaped canyon. And I was amazed at the
size and density of that jungle of scrub oaks, maples and
aspens. From above the color was a blaze of scarlet and gold
and green, with bronze tinge.

Presently I crossed a fresh bear track, so fresh that I could
see the dampness of the dark earth, the rolling of little
particles, the springing erect of bent grasses. In some places
big sections of earth, a yard wide had slipped under the feet
of this particular bear. He appeared to be working down.
Right then I wanted to go up! But I could not climb out there.
I had to go down. Soon I was under low-spreading, dense
spruces, and I had to hold on desperately to keep from
sliding. All the time naturally I kept a keen lookout for a
bear. Every stone and tree trunk resembled a bear. I decided
if I met a grizzly that I would not annoy him on that slope. I
would say: "Nice bear, I won't hurt you!" Still the situation
had some kind of charm. But to claim I was not frightened
would not be strictly truthful. I slid over the trail of that bear
into the trail of another one, and under the last big spruce on

that part of the slope I found a hollow nest of pine needles and leaves, and if that bed was not still warm then my imagination lent considerable to the moment.

Beyond this began the edge of the thicket. It was small pine at first, so close together that I had to squeeze through, and as dark as twilight. The ground was a slant of brown pine needles, so slippery, that if I could not have held on to trees and branches I never would have kept my feet. In this dark strip I had more than apprehensions. What a comfortable place to encounter an outraged or wounded grizzly bear! The manzanita thicket was preferable. But as Providence would have it I did not encounter one.

Soon I worked or wormed out of the pines into the thicket of scrub oaks, maples and aspens. The change was welcome. Not only did the slope lengthen out, but the light changed from gloom to gold. There was half a foot of scarlet, gold, bronze, red and purple leaves on the ground, and every step I made I kicked acorns about to rustle and roll. Bear sign was everywhere, tracks and trails and beds and scratches. I kept going down, and the farther down I got the lighter it grew, and more approaching a level. One glade was strangely luminous and beautiful with a blending of gold and purple light made by the sun shining through the leaves overhead down upon the carpet of leaves on the ground. Then I came into a glade that reminded me of Kipling's moonlight dance of the wild elephants. Here the leaves and fern were rolled and matted flat, smooth as if done by a huge roller. Bears and bears had lolled and slept and played there. A little below this glade was a place, shady and cool, where a seep of water came from under a bank. It looked like a herd of cattle had stamped the earth, only the tracks were bear tracks. Little ones no longer than a child's hand, and larger, up to huge tracks a foot long and almost as wide. Many were old, but some were fresh. This little spot smelled of bear so strongly that it reminded me of the bear pen in the Bronx Park Zoological Garden. I had been keen for sight of bear trails and scent of bear fur, but this was a little too much. I thought it was too much because the place was lonely and dark and absolutely silent. I went on down to the gully that ran down

the middle of the canyon. It was more open here. The sun got
through, and there were some big pines.

I could see the bluff that the Haughts had climbed so
laboriously, and now I understood why they had been so
slow. It was straight up, brush and jumbled rock, and two
hundred feet over my head. Somewhere above that bluff was
the bluff where our bear had run along.

I rested and listened for the dogs. There was no wind to
deceive me, but I imagined I heard dogs everywhere. It
seemed unwise for me to go on down the canyon, for if I did
not meet the men I would find myself lost. As it was I would
have my troubles climbing out.

I chose a part of the thicket some distance above where I
had come down, hoping to find it more open, if not less
steep, and not so vastly inhabited with bears. Lo and behold it
was worse! It was thicker, darker, wilder, steeper, and there
was, if possible, actually more bear sign. I had to pull myself
up by holding to the trees and branches. I had to rest every
few steps. I had to watch and listen all the time. Half-way up
the trunks of the aspens and oaks and maples were all bent
down-hill. They curved out and down before the rest of the
tree stood upright. And all the brush was flat, bending down
hill, and absolutely almost impassable. This feature of tree
and brush was of course caused by the weight of snow in
winter. It would have been more interesting if I had not been
so anxious to get up. I grew hotter and wetter than I had been
in the manzanitas. Moreover, what with the labor and worry
and exhaustion, my apprehensions had increased. They increased until I had to confess that I was scared. Once I heard
a rustle and pad on the leaves somewhere below. That made
matters worse. Surely I would meet a bear. I would meet him
coming down-hill! And I must never shoot a bear coming
down-hill! Buffalo Jones had cautioned me on that score, so
had Scott Teague, the bear hunter of Colorado, and so had
Haught. "Don't never shoot no ole bar comin' down hill, 'cause
if you do he'll just roll up an' pile down on you!"

I climbed until my tongue hung out and my heart was
likely to burst. Then when I had to straddle a tree to keep
from sliding down I got desperate and mad and hoped an old
grizzly would happen along to make an end to my misery.

It took me an hour to climb up that part of the slope which constituted the thicket of oak, maple and aspen. It was half-past three when finally I reached the saddle where we had shot at the grizzly. I rested as long as I dared. I had still a long way to go up that ridge to the rim, and how did I know whether or not I could surmount it?

However, a good rest helped to revive strength and spirit. Then I started. Once above the saddle I was out clear in the open, high above the canyons, and the vast basin still farther below, yet far indeed under the pine-fringed rim above. This climb was all over stone. The ridge was narrow-crested, yellow, splintered rock, with a few dwarf pines and spruces and an occasional bunch of manzanita. I did not hear a sound that I did not make myself. Whatever had become of the hounds, and the other hunters? The higher I climbed the more I liked it. After an hour I was sure that I could reach the rim by this route, and of course that stimulated me. To make sure, and allay doubt, I sat down on a high backbone of bare rock and studied the heave and bulge of ridge above me. Using my glasses I made sure that I could climb out. It would be a task equal to those of lion-hunting days with Jones, and it made me happy to realize that despite the intervening ten years I was still equal to the task.

Once assured of this I grew acute to the sensations of the hour. This was one of my especial joys of the open—to be alone high on some promontory, above wild and beautiful scenery. The sun was still an hour from setting, and it had begun to soften, to grow intense, and more golden. There were clouds and lights that promised a magnificent sunset.

So I climbed on. When I stopped to rest I would shove a stone loose and watch it heave and slide, and leap out and hurtle down, to make the dust fly, and crash into the thickets, and eventually start an avalanche that would roar down into the canyon.

The Tonto Basin seemed a vast bowl of rolling, rough, black ridges and canyons, green and dark and yellow, with the great mountain ranges enclosing it to south and west. The black-fringed promontories of the rim, bold and rugged, leagues apart, stood out over the void. The colors of autumn gleamed under the cliffs, everywhere patches of gold and long slants of green and spots of scarlet and clefts of purple.

The last benches of that ridge taxed my waning strength. I had to step up, climb up, pull myself up, by hand and knee and body. My rifle grew to weigh a ton. My cartridge belt was a burden of lead around my waist. If had been hot and wet below in the thicket I wondered what I grew on the last steps of this ridge. Yet even the toil and the pain held a keen pleasure. I did not analyze my feelings then, but it was good to be there.

The rim-rock came out to a point above me, seeming unscalable, all grown over with brush and lichen, and stunted spruce. But by hauling myself up, and crawling here, and winding under bridges of rock there, and holding to the brush, at last, panting and spent, I reached the top.

I was ready to drop on the mats of pine needles and lie there, unutterably grateful for rest, when I heard Old Tom baying, deep and ringing and close. He seemed right under the rim on the side of the ridge opposite to where I had climbed. I looked around. There was George's horse tied to a pine, and farther on my own horse Stockings.

Then I walked to the rim and looked down into the gold and scarlet thicket. Actually it seemed to me then, and always will seem, that the first object I clearly distinguished was a big black bear standing in an open aisle at the upper reach of the thicket close to the cliff. He shone black as shiny coal. He was looking down into the thicket, as if listening to the baying hound.

I could not repress an exclamation of surprise and thrilling excitement, and I uttered it as I raised my rifle. Just the instant I saw his shining fur through the circle of my rear sight he heard me and jumped, and my bullet missed him. Like a black flash he was gone around a corner of gray ledge.

"Well!" I ejaculated, suddenly weak. "After all this long day—to get a chance like that—and miss!"

All that seemed left of that long day was the sunset, out of which I could not be cheated by blunders or bad luck. Westward a glorious golden ball blazed over the rim. Above that shone an intense belt of color—Coleridge's yellow lightning—

and it extended to a bank of cloud that seemed transparent
purple, and above all this flowed a sea of purest blue sky with
fleecy sails of pink and white and rose, exquisitely flecked
with gold.

Lost indeed was I to weariness and time until the gorgeous
transformation at last ended in dull gray. I walked along the
rim, back to where I had tied my horse. He saw me and
whinnied before I located the spot. I just about had strength
enough left to straddle him. And presently through the twilight shadows I caught a bright glimmer of our camp-fire.
Supper was ready; Takahashi grinned his concern away; all the
men were waiting for me; and like the Ancient Mariner I told
my tale. As I sat to a bountiful repast regaling myself, the
talk of my companions seemed absolutely satisfying.

George Haught, on a stand at the apex of the canyon, had
heard and seen a big brown bear climbing up through the
thicket, and he had overshot and missed. R.C. had espied a
big black bear walking a slide some four hundred yards down
the canyon slope, and forgetting that he had a heavy close-
range shell in his rifle instead of one of high trajectory, he
had aimed accordingly, to undershoot half a foot and thus lose
his opportunity. Nielsen had been lost most of the day. It
seemed everywhere he heard yells and bays down in the
canyon, and once he had heard a loud rattling crash of a
heavy bear tearing through the thicket. Edd told of the fearful
climb he and his father had made, how they had shot at the
grizzly a long way off, how funny another bear had rolled
around in his bed across the canyon. But the hounds got too
tired to hold the trails late in the day. And lastly Edd said:
"When you an' Ben were smokin' the grizzly I could hear the
bullets hit close above us, an' I was sure scared stiff for fear
you'd roll him down on us. But father wasn't scared. He said,
'let the old Jasper roll down! We'll assassinate him!' "

When the old bear hunter began to tell his part in the day's
adventures my pleasure was tinglingly keen and nothing was
wanting on the moment except that my boy Romer was not
there to hear.

"Wal, shore it was an old bar day," said Haught, with
quaint satisfaction. His blue shirt, ragged and torn and black

from brush, surely attested to the truth of his words. "All told we seen five bars. Two blacks, two browns an' the old Jasper. Some of them big fellars, too. But we missed seein' the boss bar of this canyon. When Old Dan opened up first off I wanted Edd to climb thet bluff. But Edd kept goin' an' we lost our chance. Fer pretty soon we heard a bustin' of the brush. My, but thet bar was rockin' her off. He knocked the brush like a wild steer, an' he ran past us close—not a hundred yards. I never heard a heavier bar. But we couldn't see him. Then Edd started up, an' thet bluff was a wolf of a place. We was half up when I seen the grizzly thet you an' Ben smoked afterward. He was far off, but Edd an' I lammed a couple after him jest for luck. One of the pups was nippin' his heels. Think it was Big Foot. . . . Wal, thet was all of thet. We plumb busted ourselves gettin' on top of the bench to head off your bar. Only we hadn't time. Then we worried along around to the top of thet higher bluff an' there I was so played-out I thought my day had come. We kept our eyes peeled, an' pretty soon I spied a big brown bar actin' queer in an open spot across the canyon. Edd seen him too, an' we argued about what thet bar was doin'. He lay in a small open place at the foot of a spruce. He wagged his head slow an' he made as if to roll over, an' he stretched his paws, an' acted shore queer. Edd said: 'Thet bar's crippled. He's been shot by one of the boys, an' he's tryin' to get up.' But I shore didn't exactly agree with Edd. So I was for watchin' him some more. He looked like a sick bar—raisin' his head so slow an' droppin' it so slow an' sort of twistin' his body. He looked like his back had been broke an' he was tryin' to get up, but somehow I couldn't believe thet. Then he lay still an' Edd swore he was dead. Shore I got almost to believin' thet myself, when he waked up. An' then the old scoundrel slid around lazy like a tom cat by the fire, and sort of rolled on his back an' stretched. Next he slapped at himself with his paws. If he wasn't sick he was shore actin' queer with thet canyon full of crackin' guns an' bayin' hounds an' yellin' men. I begun to get suspicious. Shore he must be a dyin' bear. So I said to Edd: 'Let's bast him a couple jest fer luck.' Wal, when we shot up jumped thet sick bar quicker'n you could wink.

An' he piled into the thicket while I was goin' down after
another shell. . . . It shore was funny. Thet old Jasper never
heard the racket, an' if he heard it he didn't care. He had a
bed in thet sunny spot an' he was foolin' around, playin' with
himself like a kitten. Playin'! An' Edd reckoned he was dyin'
an' I come shore near bein' fooled. The old Jasper! We'll
assassinate him fer thet!''

VIII

Five more long arduous days we put in chasing bears under
the rim from Pyle's Canyon to Verde Canyon. In all we
started over a dozen bears. But I was inclined to think that we
chased the same bears over and over from one canyon to
another. The boys got a good many long-range shots, which,
however, apparently did no damage. But as for me, the
harder and farther I tramped and the longer I watched and
waited the less opportunity had I to shoot a bear.

This circumstance weighed heavily upon the spirits of my
comrades. They wore their boots out, as well as the feet of
the hounds, trying to chase a bear somewhere near me. And
wherever I stayed or went there was the place the bears
avoided. Edd and Neilsen lost flesh in this daily toil. Haught
had gloomy moments. But as for me the daily ten- or fifteen-
mile grind up and down the steep craggy slopes had at last
trained me back to my former vigorous condition, and I was
happy. No one knew it, not even R. C., but the fact was I
really did not care in the least whether I shot a bear or not.
Bears were incidental to my hunting trip. I had not a little
secret glee over the praise accorded me by Copple and Haught
and Nielsen, who all thought that the way I persevered was
remarkable. They would have broken their necks to get me a
bear. At times R. C. when he was tired fell victim to discouragement and he would make some caustic remark: ''I don't
know about you. I've a hunch you like to pack a rifle because
it's heavy. And you go dreaming along! Sometime a bear will
rise up and swipe you one!''

Takahashi passed from concern to grief over what he considered my bad luck: ''My goodnish! No see bear to-day? . . .

Maybe more better luck to-morrow." If I could have had some of Takahashi's luck I would scarcely have needed to leave camp. He borrowed Nielsen's 30-40 rifle and went hunting without ever having shot it. He rode the little buck-skin mustang, that, remarkable to state, had not yet thrown him or kicked him. And on that occasion he led the mustang back to camp with a fine two-point buck on the saddle. "Camp need fresh meat," said the Jap, with his broad smile. "I go hunt. Ride along old road. Soon nice fat deer walk out from bush. Twenty steps away—maybe. I get off. I no want kill deer so close, so I walk on him. Deer he no scared. He jump off few steps—stick up his ears—look at horse all same like he thought him deer too. I no aim gun from shoulder. I just shoot. No good. Deer he run. I aim then—way front of him—shoot—deer he drop right down dead. . . . Aw, easy to get deer!"

I would have given a great deal to have been able to describe Haught's face when the Jap finished his story of killing that deer. But such feat was beyond human ingenuity. "Wal," ejaculated the hunter, "in all my days raslin' round with fools packin' guns I never seen the likes of thet. No wonder the Japs licked the Russians!" This achievement of Takahashi's led me to suggest his hunting bear with us. "Aw sure—I kill bear too," he said. Takahashi outwalked and outclimbed us all. He never made detours. He climbed straight up or descended straight down. Copple and Edd were com-pelled to see him take the lead and keep it. What a wonderful climber! What a picture the sturdy little brown man made, carrying a rifle longer than himself, agile and sure-footed as a goat, perfectly at home in the depths or on the heights! I took occasion to ask Takahashi if he had been used to mountain climbing in Japan. "Aw sure. I have father own whole mountain more bigger here. I climb high—saw wood. Leetle boy so big." And he held his hand about a foot from the ground. Thus for me every day brought out some further interesting or humorous or remarkable feature pertaining to Takahashi.

The next day added to the discouragement of my party. We drove Verde Canyon and ran the dogs into a nest of steel-traps. Big Foot was caught in one, and only the remarkable size and strength of his leg saved it from being broken. Nielsen found a poor, miserable, little fox in a trap, where it had been for days, and was nearly dead. Edd found a dead skunk in another. He had to call the hounds in. We returned to camp. That night was really the only cheerless one the men spent around the fire. They did not know what to do. Manifestly with trappers in a locality there could be no more bear chasing. Disappointment perched upon the countenances of the Haughts and Copple and Nielsen. I let them all have their say. Finally Haught spoke up: "Wal, fellars, I'm figgerin' hard an' I reckon here's my stand. We jest naturally have to get Doc an' his brother a bear apiece. Shore I expected we'd get 'em a couple. Now, them traps we seen are all small. We didn't run across no bear traps. An' I reckon we can risk the dogs. We'll shore go back an' drive Verde Canyon. We can't do no worse than break a leg for a dog. I'd hate to see thet happen to Old Dan or Tom. But we'll take a chance."

After that there fell a moment's silence. I could see from Edd's face what a serious predicament this was. Nothing was plainer than his fondness for the hounds. Finally he said: "Sure. We'll take a chance." Their devotion to my interest, their simple earnestness, warmed me to them. But not for all the bears under the rim would I have been wittingly to blame for Old Dan or Old Tom breaking a leg.

"Men, I've got a better plan," I said. "We'll let the bears here rest for a spell. Supplies are about gone. Let's go back to Beaver Dam camp for a week or so. Rest up the hounds. Maybe we'll have a storm and a cold snap that will improve conditions. Then we'll come back here. I'll send Haught down to buy off the trappers. I'll pay them to spring their traps and let us have our hunt without risk of the hounds."

Instantly the men brightened. The insurmountable obstacles seemed to melt away. Only Haught demurred a little at additional and unreasonable expense for me. But I cheered him over this hindrance, and the last part of that evening round the camp-fire was very pleasant.

The following morning we broke camp, and all rode off, except Haught and his son George, who remained to hunt a strayed burro. "Reckon thet lion eat him. My best burro. He was the one your boy was always playin' with. I'm goin' to assassinate thet lion."

On the way back to BeaverDam camp I happened to be near Takahashi when he dismounted to shoot at a squirrel. Returning to get back in the saddle the Jap forgot to approach the mustang from the proper side. There was a scuffle between Takahashi and the mustang as to which of them should possess the bridle. The Jap lost this argument. Edd had to repair the broken bridle. I watched Takahashi and could see that he did not like the mustang any better than the mustang liked him. Soon the struggle for supremacy would take place between this ill assorted rider and horse. I rather felt inclined to favor the latter; nevertheless it was only fair to Takahashi to admit that his buckskin-colored mustang had some mean traits.

In due time I arrived at our permanent camp, to be the last to get in. Lee and his father welcomed us as familiar faces in a strange land. As I dismounted I heard heavy thuds and cracks accompanied by fierce utterances in a foreign tongue. These sounds issued from the corral.

"I'll bet the Jap got what was coming to him," declared Lee.

We all ran toward the corral. A bunch of horses obstructed our view, and we could not see Takahashi until we ran round to the other side. The Jap had the buckskin mustang up in a corner and was vigorously whacking him with a huge pole. Not by any means was the mustang docile. Like a mule, he kicked. "Hey George," yelled Lee, "don't kill him! What's the matter?"

Takahashi slammed the mustang one parting blow, which broke the club, and then he turned to us. We could see from dust and dirt on his person that he had lately been in close relation to the earth. Takahashi's face was pale except for a great red lump on his jaw. The Jap was terribly angry. He seemed hurt, too. With a shaking hand he pointed to the bruise on his jaw.

"Look what he do!" exclaimed Takahashi. "He throw me off! . . . He kick me awful hard! I kill him sure next time."

Lee and I managed to conceal our mirth until our irate cook
had gotten out of hearing. "Look—what—he—do!" choked
Lee, imitating Takahashi. Then Lee broke out and roared. I
had to join him. I laughed till I cried. My family and friends
severely criticise this primitive trait of mine, but I can not
help it. Later I went to Takahashi and asked to examine his
jaw, fearing it might have been broken. This fear of mine,
however, was unfounded. Moreover the Jap had recovered
from his pain and anger. "More better now," he said, with a
grin. "Maybe my fault anyhow."

Next day we rested, and the following morning was so fine
and clear and frosty that we decided to go hunting. We rode
east on the way to See Lake through beautiful deep forest.

I saw a deer trotting away into the woods. I jumped off,
jerked out my gun, and ran hard, hoping to see him in an
opening. Lo! I jumped a herd of six more deer, some of them
bucks. They plunged everywhere. I tried frantically to get my
sights on one. All I could aim at was bobbing ears. I shot
twice, and of course missed. R. C. shot four times, once at a
running buck, and three at a small deer that he said was flying!

Here Copple and Haught caught up with us. We went on,
and turned off the road on the blazed trail to See Lake. It was
pretty open forest, oaks and scattered pines, and a few spruce.
The first park we came to was a flat grassy open, with places
where deer licked the bare earth. Copple left several pounds
of salt in these spots. R. C. and I went up to the upper end
where he had seen deer before. No deer this day! But saw
three turkeys, one an old gobbler. We lost sight of them.

Then Copple and R. C. went one way and Haught and I
another. We went clear to the rim, and then circled around,
and eventually met R. C. and Copple. Together we started to
return. Going down a little draw we found water, and R. C.
saw where a rock had been splashed with water and was still
wet. Then I saw a turkey track upon this rock. We slipped up
the slope, with me in the lead. As I came out on top, I saw
five big gobblers feeding. Strange how these game birds
thrilled me! One saw me and started to run. Like a streak!
Another edged away into pines. Then I espied one with his
head and neck behind a tree and he was scratching away in

the pine needles. I could not see much of him, but that little was not running, so I drew down upon him, tried to aim fine, and fired. He leaped up with a roar of wings, sending the dust and needles flying. Then he dropped back, and like a flash darted into a thicket.

Another flew straight out of the glade. Another ran like an ostrich in the same direction. I tried to get the sights on him. In vain!

R. C. and Copple chased these two speeding turkeys, and Haught and I went the other way. We could find no trace of ours. And we returned to our horses.

Presently we heard shots. One—two—three—pause—then several more. And finally more, to a total number of fifteen. I could not stand that and I had to hurry back into the woods. I saw one old gobbler running wildly around as if lost, but I did not shoot at him because he seemed to be in line with the direction which R. C. and Copple had taken. I should have run after him until he went some other way.

I could not find the hunters, and returned to our resting place, which they had reached ahead of me. They had a turkey each, gobblers about two years old Copple said.

R. C. told an interesting story of how he had run in the direction the two turkeys had taken, and suddenly flushed thirty or forty more, some big old gobblers, but mostly young. They scattered and ran. He followed as fast as he could, shooting a few times. Copple could not keep up with him, but evidently had a few shots himself. R. C. chased most of the flock across several small canyons, till he came to a deep canyon. Here he hoped to make a killing when the turkeys ran up the far slope. But they flew across! And he heard them clucking over there. He crossed, and went on cautiously. Once he saw three turkey heads sticking above a log. Wise old gobblers! They protected their bodies while they watched for him. He tried to get sidewise to them but they ran off. Then he followed until once more he heard clucking.

Here he sat down, just beyond the edge of a canyon, and began to call with his turkey wing. It thrilled him to hear his calls answered on all sides. Here was a wonderful opportunity. He realized that the turkeys were mostly young and scattered, and frightened, and wanted to come together. He kept calling, and as they neared him on all sides he felt something more than the zest of hunting. Suddenly Copple began to shoot. Spang! Spang! Spang! R. C. saw the dust fly under one turkey. He heard the bullet glance. The next shot killed a turkey. Then R. C. yelled that *he* was no turkey! Then of that scattering flock he managed to knock over one for himself.

Copple had been deceived by the call of an amateur. That flattered R. C., but he was keenly disappointed that Copple had spoiled the situation.

During the day the blue sky was covered by thin flying clouds that gradually thickened and darkened. The wind grew keener and colder, and veered to the southwest. We all said storm. There was no sunset. Darker clouds rolled up, obliterating the few stars.

We went to bed. Long after that I heard the swell and roar and crash and lull of the wind in the pines, a sound I had learned to love in Buckskin Forest with Buffalo Jones. At last I fell asleep.

Sometime in the night I awoke. A fine rain was pattering on the tent. It grew stronger. After a while I went to sleep again. Upon awakening I found that the storm had struck with a vengeance. It was dull gray daylight, foggy, cold, windy, with rain and snow.

I got up, built a fire, puttered around the tents to loosen the ground ropes, and found that it was nipping cold. My fingers ached. The storm increased, and then we fully appreciated the tent with stove. The rain roared on the tent roof, and all morning the wind increased, and the air grew colder. I hoped it would turn to snow.

Soon indeed we were storm bound. On the third day the wind reached a very high velocity. The roar in the pines was stupendous. Many times I heard the dull crash of a falling tree. With the ground saturated by the copious rain, and the fury of the storm blast, a great many trees were felled. That night it rained all night, not so hard, but steadily, now low, now vigorously. After morning snow began to fall. But it did not lay long. After a while it changed to sleet. At times the dark, lowering, scurrying clouds broke to emit a flare of sunshine and to show a patch of blue. These last however were soon obscured by the scudding gray pall. Every now and then a little shower of rain or sleet pattered on the tents. We looked for a clearing up.

That night about eight o'clock the clouds vanished and stars shone. In the night the wind rose and roared. In the morning all was dark, cloudy, raw, cold. But the wind had died out, and there were spots of blue showing. These spots enlarged as the morning advanced, and about nine the sun, golden and dazzling, beautified the forest. "Bright sunny days will soon come again!"

It was good to have hope and belief in that.

All the horses but Don Carlos weathered the storm in good shape. Don lost considerable weight. He had never before been left with hobbled feet to shift for himself in a prolonged storm of rain, sleet and snow. He had cut himself upon brush, and altogether had fared poorly. He showed plainly that he had been neglected. Don was the only horse I had ever known of that did not welcome the wilderess and companionship with his kind.

We rested the following day, and on the next we packed and started back to Dude Creek. It was a cold, raw, bitter day, with a gale from the north, such a day as I could never have endured had I not become hardened. As it was I almost enjoyed wind and cold. What a transformation in the woods! The little lakes were all frozen over; pines, moss, grass were white with frost. The sear days had come. Not a leaf showed in the aspen and maple thickets. The scrub oaks were shaggy and ragged, gray as the rocks. From the rim the slopes looked steely and dark, thinned out, showing the rocks and slides.

When we reached our old camp in Barber Shop Canyon we were all glad to see Haught's lost burro waiting for us there. Not a scratch showed on the shaggy lop-eared little beast. Haught for once unhobbled a burro and set it free without a parting kick. Nielsen too had observed this omission on Haught's part. Nielsen was a desert man and he knew burros. He said prospectors were inclined to show affection for burros

by sundry cuffs and kicks. And Nielsen told me a story about
Haught. It seemed the bear hunter was noted for that habit of
kicking burros. Sometimes he was in fun and sometimes,
when burros were obstinate, he was in earnest. Upon one
occasion a big burro stayed away from camp quite a long
time—long enough to incur Haught's displeasure. He needed
the burro and could not find it, and all he could do was to
hunt for it. Upon returning to camp there stood the big gray
burro, lazy and fat, just as if he had been perfectly well
behaved. Haught put a halter on the burro, using strong
language the while, and then he proceeded to exercise his
habit of kicking burros. He kicked this one until its fat belly
gave forth sounds exceedingly like a bass drum. When Haught
had ended his exercise he tied up the burro. Presently a man
came running into Haught's camp. He appeared alarmed. He
was wet and panting. Haught recognized him as a miner from
a mine nearby. "Hey Haught," panted the miner, "hev you
seen—your gray burro—thet big one—with white face?"

"Shore, there he is," replied Haught. "Son of a gun jest
rustled home."

The miner appeared immensely relieved. He looked and
looked at the gray burro as if to make sure it was there, in the
solid flesh, a really tangible object. Then he said: "We was
all afeared you'd kick the stuffin's out of him! . . . Not an
hour ago he was over at the mine, an' he ate five sticks of
dynamite! Five sticks! For Lord's sake handle him gently!"

Haught turned pale and suddenly sat down. "Ahuh!" was
all he said. But he had a strange hunted look. And not for a
long time did he ever again kick a burro!

Hunting conditions at Dude Creek had changed greatly to
our benefit. The trappers had pulled up stakes and gone to
some other section of the country. There was not a hunting
party within fifteen miles of our camp. Leaves and acorns
were all down; trails were soft and easy to travel; no dust rose
on the southern slopes; the days were cold and bright; in
every pocket and ravine there was water for the dogs; from
any stand we could see into the shaggy thickets where before
all we could see was a blaze of color.

In three days we drove Pyle's Canyon, Dude Creek, and the small adjoining canyons, chasing in all nine bears, none of which ran anywhere near R. C. or me. Old Dan gave out and had to rest every other day. So the gloom again began to settle thick over the hopes of my faithful friends. Long since, as in 1918, I had given up expectations of bagging a bear or a buck. For R. C., however, my hopes still held good. At least I did not give up for him. But he shared somewhat the feelings of the men. Still he worked harder than ever, abandoning the idea of waiting on one of the high stands, and took to the slopes under the rim where he toiled down and up all day long. It pleased me to learn, presently, that this activity, strenuous as it was, became a source of delight to him. How different such toil was from waiting and watching on the rim!

On November first, a bitter cold morning, with ice in the bright air, we went back to Pyle's Canyon, and four of us went down with Edd and the hounds. We had several chases, and about the middle of the forenoon I found myself alone, making tracks for the saddle overlooking Bear Canyon. Along the south side of the slope, in the still air the sun was warm, but when I got up onto the saddle, in an exposed place, the wind soon chilled me through. I would keep my stand until I nearly froze, then I had to go around to the sunny sheltered side and warm up. The hounds finally got within hearing again, and eventually appeared to be in Bear Canyon, toward the mouth. I decided I ought to go round the ridge on the east side and see if I could hear better. Accordingly I set off, and the hard going over the sunny slope was just what I needed. When I reached the end of the ridge, under the great dome, I heard the hounds below me, somewhat to my left. Running and plowing down through the brush I gained the edge of the bluff, just in time to see some of the hounds passing on. They had run a bear through that thicket, and if I had been there sooner I would have been fortunate. But too late! I worked around the head of this canyon and across a wide promontory. Again I heard the hounds right under me. They came nearer, and soon I heard rolling rocks and cracking brush, which sounds I believed were made by a bear. After a while I espied Old Tom and Rock working up the canyon on a trail. Then I was sure I would get a shot. Presently, however, Old Tom left the trail and started back. Rock came on, climbed the ridge, and hearing me call he came to me. I went over to the place where he had climbed out and found an enormous bear track pointing in the direction the hounds had come. They had back-trailed him. Rock went back to join Old Tom. Some of the pack were baying at a great rate in the mouth of the next canyon. But an impassable cliff prevented me from working around to that point. So I had to address myself to the long steep climb upward. I had not gone far when I crossed the huge bear track that Rock and Old Tom had given up. This track was six inches wide and ten inches long. The bear that had made it had come down this very morning from over the ridge east of Bear Canyon. I trailed him up this ridge, over the steepest and roughest and wildest part of it, marveling at the enormous steps and jumps he made, and at the sagacity which caused him to choose this route instead of the saddle trail where I had waited so long. His track led up nearly to the rim and proved how he had climbed over the most rugged break in the ridge. Indeed he was one of the wise old scoundrels. When I reached camp I learned that Sue and several more of the hounds had held a bear for some time in the box of the canyon just beyond where I had to give up. Edd and Nielsen were across this canyon, unable to go farther, and then yelled themselves hoarse, trying to call some of us. I asked Edd if he saw the bear. "Sure did," replied Edd. "One of them long, lean, hungry cinnamons." I had to laugh, and told how near I had come to meeting a bear that was short, fat, and heavy: "One of the old Jasper scoundrels!"

That night at dark the wind still blew a gale, and seemed more bitterly cold. We hugged the camp-fire. My eyes smarted from the smoke and my face grew black. Before I went to bed I toasted myself so thoroughly that my clothes actually burned me as I lay down. But they heated the blankets and that made my bed snug and soon I was in the land of dreams. During the night I awoke. The wind had lulled. The canopy above was clear, cold, starry, beautiful. When we rolled out the mercury showed ten above zero. Perhaps looking at the thermometer made us feel colder, but in any event we would have had to move about to keep warm. I built a fire and my hands were blocks of ice when I got the blaze stirring.

That day, so keen and bright, so wonderful with its clarity of atmosphere and the breath of winter through the pines, promised to be as exciting as it was beautiful. Maybe this day R. C. would bag a bear!

When we reached the rim the sunrise was just flushing the purple basin, flooding with exquisite gold and rose light the slumberous shadows. What a glorious wilderness to greet the eye at sunrise! I suffered a pang to realize what men missed—what I had to miss so many wonderful mornings.

We had made our plan. The hounds had left a bear in the second canyon east of Dude. Edd started down. Copple and Takahashi followed to hug the lower slopes. Nielsen and Haught and George held to the rim to ride east in case the hounds chased a bear that way. And R. C. and I were to try to climb out and down a thin rock-crested ridge which, so far as Haught knew, no one had ever been on.

Looked at from above this ridge was indeed a beautiful and rugged backbone of rock, sloping from the rim, extending far out and down—a very narrow knife-edge extended promontory, green with cedar and pine, yellow and gray with its crags and rocks. A craggy point comparable to some of those in the Grand Canyon! We had to study a way to get across the first deep fissures, and eventually descended far under the crest and climbed back. It was desperately hard work, for we had so little time. R. C. was to be at the middle of that ridge and I at the end in an hour. Like Trojans we worked. Some slippery pine-needle slopes we had to run across, for light quick steps were the only means of safe travel. And that was not safe! When we surmounted to the crest we found a jumble of weathered rocks ready to slide down on either side. Slabs, pyramids, columns, shale, rocks of all shapes except round, lay toppling along the heaved ridge. It seemed the whole ridge was ready to thunder down into the abyss. Half a mile down and out from the rim we felt lost, marooned. But there was something splendidly thrilling in our conquest of that narrow upflung edge of mountain. Twice R. C. thought we would have to abandon further progress, but I found ways

to go on. How lonely and wild out there! No foot save an
Indian's had ever trod those gray rocks or brown mats of pine
needles.

Before we reached the dip or saddle where R. C. was to
make his stand the hounds opened up far below. The morning
was perfectly still, an unusual occurrence there along the rim.
What wild music! Then Edd's horn pealed out, ringing melody, a long blast keen and clear, telling us above that he had
started a bear. That made us hurry. We arrived at the head of
an incline leading down to R. C.'s stand. As luck would have
it the place was ideal for a bear, but risky for a hunter. A bear
could come four ways without being seen until he was close
enough to kill a man. We hurried on. At the saddle there was
a broad bear trail with several other trails leading into it.
Suddenly R. C. halted me with a warning finger. "Listen!"

I heard a faint clear rifle shot. Then another, and a fainter
yell. We stood there and counted eleven more shots. Then the
bay of the hounds seemed to grow closer. We had little time
to pick and choose stands. I had yet to reach the end of the
ridge—a task requiring seven-league boots. But I took time to
choose the best possible stand for R. C. and that was one
where a bear approaching from only the east along under the
ridge could surprise him. In bad places like this we always
tried to have our minds made up what to do and where to get
in case of being charged by a wounded grizzly. In this
instance there was not a rock or a tree near at hand. "R. C.
you'll have to stand your ground and kill him, that's all," I
declared, grimly. "But it's quiet. You can hear a bear coming. If you do hear one—wait—and make sure your first shot
lets him down."

"Don't worry. I could hear a squirrel coming over this
ground," replied R. C.

Then I went on, not exactly at ease in mind, but stirred and
thrilled to the keen charged atmosphere. I had to go around
under the base of a rocky ledge, over rough ground. Presently
I dropped into a bear trail, well trodden. I followed it to a
corner of cliff where it went down. Then I kept on over loose
rock and bare earth washed deep in ruts. I had to leap these.
Perhaps in ten minutes I had traveled a quarter of a mile or

less. Then *spang!* R. C.'s rifle-shot halted me. So clear and sharp, so close, so startling! I was thrilled, delighted—he had gotten a shot. I wanted to yell my pleasure. My blood warmed and my nerves tingled. Swiftly my thoughts ran—bad luck was nothing—a man had only to stick at a thing—what a fine, sharp, wonderful day for adventure! How the hounds bayed! Had R. C. sighted a bear somewhere below? Suddenly the still air split—*spang!* R. C.'s second shot gave me a shock. My breast contracted. I started back. "Suppose it was a grizzly—on that bad side!" I muttered. *Spang!* . . . I began to run. A great sweeping wave of emotion charged over me, swelling all my veins to the bursting point. *Spang!* My heart came to my throat. Leaping the ruts, bounding like a sheep from rock to rock, I covered my back tracks. All inside me seemed to flutter, yet I felt cold and hard—a sickening sense of reproach that I had left my brother in a bad position. *Spang!* His fifth and last shot followed swiftly after the fourth—too swift to be accurate. So hurriedly a man would act in close quarters. R. C. now had an empty rifle! . . . Like a flash I crossed that slope leading to the rocks, and tore around the cliff at such speed that it was a wonder I did not pitch down and break my neck. How long—how terribly long I seemed in reaching the corner of cliff! Then I plunged to a halt with eyes darting everywhere.

R. C. was not in sight. The steep curved neck of slope seemed all rocks, all trees, all brush. Then I heard a wild hoarse bawl and a loud crashing of brush. My gaze swerved to an open spot. A patch of manzanita seemed to blur round a big bear, standing up, fighting the branches, threshing and growling. But where was R. C.? Fearfully my gaze peered near and all around this wounded bear. "Hey there!" I yelled with all my might.

R. C.'s answer was another *spang.* I heard the bullet hit the bear. It must have gone clear through him for I saw bits of fur and manzanita fly. The bear plunged out of the bushes—out of my sight. How he crashed the brush—rolled the rocks! I listened. Down and down he crashed. Then the sound changed somewhat. He was rolling. At last that thumping sound ceased, and after it the roll of rocks.

"Are you—all right?" I shouted.

Then, after a moment that made me breathless, I heard R. C. laugh, a little shakily. "Sure am. . . . Did you see him?"

"Yes. I think he's your bear."

"I'm afraid he's got away. The hounds took another bear down the canyon. What'll we do?"

"Come on down," I said.

Fifty yards or more down the slope we met. I showed him a great splotch of blood on a flat stone. "We'll find him not far down," I said. So we slid and crawled, and held to brush and rocks, following that bloody trail until we came to a ledge. From there I espied the bear lodged against a manzanita bush. He lay on his back, all four paws extended, and he was motionless. R. C. and I sat down right there on the ledge.

"Looks pretty big—black and brown—mostly brown," I said. "I'm glad, old man, you stuck it out."

"Big! . . ." exclaimed R. C. with that same peculiar little laugh. "He doesn't look big *now*. But up there he looked like a hill. . . . What do you think? He came up that very way you told me to look out for. And if I hadn't had ears he'd got right on me. As it was, when I heard little rolling stones, and then saw him, he was almost on a level with me. My nerve was all right. I knew I had him. And I made sure of my first shot. I knocked him flat. But he got up—let out an awful snarl—and plunged my way. I can't say I know he charged me. Only it was just the same as if he had! . . . I knocked him down again and this time he began to kick and jump down the slope. That was my best shot. Think I missed him the next three. You see I had time to get shaky. If he had kept coming at me—good night! . . . I had trouble loading. But when I got ready again I ran down and saw him in that bush. Wasn't far from him then. When he let out that bawl he saw me. I don't know much about bears, but I know he wanted to get at me. And I'm sure of what he'd have done. . . . I didn't miss my last shot."

We sat there a while longer, slowly calming down. Wonderful indeed had been some of the moments of thrill, but there had been others not conducive to happiness. Why do men yearn for adventure in wild moments and regret the risks and spilled blood afterward?

IX

The hounds enjoyed a well-earned rest the next day. R. C. and I, behind Haught's back, fed them all they could eat. The old hunter had a fixed idea that dogs should be kept lean and hungry so they would run bears the better. Perhaps he was right. Only I could not withstand Old Dan and Old Tom as they limped to me, begging and whining. Yet not even sore feet and hunger could rob these grand old hounds of their dignity. For an hour that morning I sat beside them in a sunny spot.

In the afternoon Copple took me on a last deer hunt for that trip. We rode down the canyon a mile, and climbed out on the west slope. Haught had described this country as a "wolf" to travel. He used that word to designate anything particularly tough. We found the ridge covered with a dense forest, in places a matted jungle of pine saplings. These thickets were impenetrable. Heavy snows had bent the pines so that they grew at an angle. We found it necessary to skirt these thickets, and at that, sometimes had to cut our way through with our little axes. Hunting was scarcely possible under such conditions. Still we did not see any deer tracks.

Eventually we crossed this ridge, or at least the jungle part of it, and got lower down into hollows and swales full of aspens. Copple recognized country he had hunted before. We made our way up a long shallow hollow that ended in an open where lay the remains of an old log cabin, and corrals. From under a bluff bubbled a clear beautiful spring. Copple looked all around slowly, with strange expression, and at last, dismounting he knelt to drink of the spring.

"Ah-h-good!" he exclaimed, after a deep draught. "Get down an' drink. Snow water an' it never goes dry."

Indeed it was so cold it made my teeth ache, and so pure and sweet that I drank until I could hold no more. Deer and cat and bear tracks showed along the margin of clean sand.

Lower down were fresh turkey tracks. A lonely spring in the woods visited by wild game! This place was singularly picturesque and beautiful. The purest drinking water is found in wild forest or on mountains. Men, cities, civilization contaminate waters that are not isolated.

Copple told me a man named Mitchell had lived in that lonely place thirty years ago. Copple, as a boy, had worked for him—had ridden wild bronchos and roped wild steers in that open, many and many a day. Something of unconscious pathos showed in Copple's eyes as he gazed around, and in his voice. We all hear the echoing footsteps of the past years! In those days Copple said the ranch was overrun by wild game, and wild horses too.

We rode on westward, to come out at length on the rim of a magnificent canyon. It was the widest and deepest and wildest gorge I had come across in this country. So deep that only a faint roar of running water reached our ears! The slopes were too steep for man, let alone a horse; and the huge cliffs and giant spruces gave it a singularly rugged appearance. We saw deer on the opposite slope. Copple led along the edge, searching for traces of an old trail where Mitchell used to drive cattle across. We did not find a trail, but we found a place where Copple said one used to be. I could see no signs of it. Here leading his horse with one hand and wielding his little axe with the other Copple started down. For my part I found going down remarkably easy. The only trouble I had was to hold on, so I would not go down like a flash. Stockings, my horse, had in a few weeks become a splendid traveler in the forest. He had learned to restrain his spirit and use his intelligence. Wherever I led he would go and that without any fear. There is something fine in constant association with an intelligent horse under such circumstances. In bad places Stockings braced his forefeet, sat on his haunches, and slid, sometimes making me jump to get out of his way. We found the canyon bed a narrow notch, darkly rich and green, full of the melody of wild birds and murmuring brook, with huge rocks all stained gold and russet, and grass as high as our knees. Frost still lingered in the dark, cool, shady retreat; and where the sun struck a narrow strip of the gorge there was warm, sweet, dry breath of the forest. But for the most part, down here all was damp, dank, cool shadow where sunshine never reached, and where the smells were of dead leaves and wet moss and ferns and black rich earth.

Impossible we found it to ascend the other slope where we had seen the deer, so we had to ride up the canyon, a matter greatly to my liking. Copple thought I was hunting with him, but really, except to follow him, I did not think of the meaning of his slow wary advance. Only a few more days had I to roam the pine-scented forest. That ride up this deep gorge was rich in sensation. Sun and sky and breeze and forest encompassed me. The wilderness was all about me; and I regretted when the canyon lost its splendid ruggedness, and became like the others I had traversed, and at last grew to be a shallow grassy ravine, with patches of gray aspens along the tiny brook.

As we climbed out once more, this time into an open, beautiful pine forest, with little patches of green thicket, I seemed to have been drugged by the fragrance and the color and the beauty of the wild. For when Copple called low and sharp: "Hist!" I stared uncomprehendingly at him.

"Deer!" he whispered, pointing. "Get off an' smoke 'em up!"

Something shot through me—a different kind of thrill. Ahead in the open I saw gray, graceful, wild forms trotting away. Like a flash I slid off my horse and jerked out my rifle. I ran forward a few steps. The deer had halted—were gazing at us with heads up and ears high. What a wild beautiful picture! As I raised my rifle they seemed to move and vanish in the green. The hunter in me, roused at last, anathematized my miserable luck. I ran ahead another few steps, to be halted by Copple. "Buck!" he called, sharply. "Hurry!" Then, farther on in the open, out in the sunlight, I saw a noble stag, moving, trotting toward us. Keen, hard, fierce in my intensity, I aligned the sights upon his breast and fired. Straight forward and high he bounded, to fall with a heavy thud.

Copple's horse, startled by my shot, began to snort and plunge. "Good shot," yelled Copple. "He's our meat."

What possessed me I knew not, but I ran ahead of Copple.

My eyes searched avidly the bush-dotted ground for my quarry. The rifle felt hot in my tight grip. All inside me was a tumult—eager, keen, wild excitement. The great pines, the green aisles leading away into the woods, the shadows under the thickets, the pine-pitch tang of the air, the loneliness of that lonely forest—all these seemed familiar, sweet, beautiful, things mine alone, things seen and smelled and felt before, things . . . Then suddenly I ran right upon my deer, lying motionless, dead I thought. He appeared fairly large, with three-point antlers. I heard Copple's horse thudding the soft earth behind me, and I yelled: "I got him, Ben." That was a moment of exultation.

It ended suddenly. Something halted me. My buck, now scarcely fifteen feet from me, began to shake and struggle. He raised his head, uttering a choking gasp. I heard the flutter of blood in his throat. He raised himself on his front feet and lifted his head high, higher, until his nose pointed skyward and his antlers lay back upon his shoulders. Then a strong convulsion shook him. I heard the shuddering wrestle of his whole body. I heard the gurgle and flow of blood. Saw the smoke of fresh blood and smelled it! I saw a small red spot in his gray breast where my bullet had struck. I saw a great bloody gaping hole on his rump where the .30 Gov't expanding bullet had come out. From end to end that bullet had torn! Yet he was not dead. Straining to rise again!

I saw, felt all this in one flashing instant. And as swiftly my spirit changed. What I might have done I never knew, but most likely I would have shot him through the brain. Only a sudden action of the stag paralyzed all my force. He lowered his head. He saw me. And dying, with lungs and heart and bowels shot to shreds, he edged his stiff front feet toward me, he dragged his afterquarters, he slid, he flopped, he skittered convulsively at me. No fear in the black, distended, wild eyes!

Only hate, only terrible, wild, unquenchable spirit to live long enough to kill me! I saw it. He meant to kill me. How magnificent, how horrible this wild courage! My eyes seemed riveted upon him, as he came closer, closer. He gasped. Blood sputtered from his throat. But more terrible than agony, than imminent death was the spirit of this wild beast to slay its enemy. Inch by inch he skidded closer to me, with a convulsive quivering awful to see. No veil of the past, no scale of civilization between beast and man then! Enemies as old as the earth! I had shot him to eat, and he would kill me before he died. For me the moment was monstrous. No hunter was I then, but a man stricken by the spirit and mystery of life, by the agony and terror of death, by the awful strange sense that this stag would kill me.

But Copple galloped up, and drawing his revolver, he shot the deer through the head. It fell in a heap.

"Don't ever go close to a crippled deer," admonished my comrade, as he leaped off his horse. "I saw a fellow once that was near killed by a buck he'd taken for dead. . . . Strange the way this buck half stood up. Reckon he meant bad, but he was all in. You hit him plumb center."

"Yes, Ben, it was—strange," I replied, soberly. I caught Copple's keen dark glance studying me. "When you open him up—see what my bullet did, will you?"

"All right. Help me hang him to a snag here," returned Copple, as he untied his lasso.

When we got the deer strung up I went off into the woods, and sat on a log, and contended with a queer sort of sickness until it passed away. But it left a state of mind that I knew would require me to probe into myself, and try to understand once and for all time this blood-thirsty tendency of man to kill. It would force me to try to analyze the psychology of hunting. Upon my return to Copple I found he had the buck ready to load upon his horse. His hands were bright red. He was wiping his hunting-knife on a bunch of green pine needles.

"That 150-grain soft-nose bullet is some executioner," he declared, forcefully. "Your bullet mushroomed just after it went into his breast. It tore his lung to pieces, cut open his heart, made a mess of kidneys an' paunch, an' broke his spine. . . . An' look at this hole where it came out!"

I helped Copple heave the load on his saddle and tie it securely, and I got my hands red at the job, but I did not really look at the buck again. And upon our way back to camp I rode in the lead all the way. We reached camp before sunset, where I had to endure the felicitations of R. C. and my comrades, all of whom were delighted that at last I had gotten a buck. Takahashi smiled all over his broad brown face. "My goodnish! I awful glad! Nice fat deer!"

That night I lay awake a long time, and though aware of the moan of the wind in the pines and the tinkle of the brook, and the melancholy hoot of an owl, and later the still, sad, black silence of the midnight hours, I really had no pleasure in them. My mind was active.

Boys are inherently cruel. The games they play, at least those they invent, instinctively partake of some element of brute nature. They chase, they capture, they imprison, they torture, and they kill. No secret rendezvous of a boy's pirate gang ever failed to be soaked with imaginary blood! And what group of boys have not played at being pirates? The Indian games are worse—scalping, with red-hot cinders thrown upon the bleeding head, and the terrible running of the gauntlet, and burning at the stake.

What youngster has not made wooden knives to spill the blood of his pretended enemies? Little girls play with dolls, and with toy houses, and all the implements of making a home; but sweet and dear as the little angels are they love a boy's game, and if they can through some lucky accident participate in one it is to scream and shudder and fight, indeed like the females of the species. No break here between these little mothers of doll-babies and the bloody mothers of the French Revolution, or of dusky, naked, barbarian children of a primitive day!

Boys love the chase. And that chase depends upon environment. For want of wild game they will harry a poor miserable tom-cat with sticks and stones. I belonged once to a gang of young ruffians who chased the neighbor's chickens, killed them with clubs, and cooked them in tin cans, over a hidden fire. Boys love nothing so much as to chase a squirrel or a frightened little chipmunk back and forth along a rail fence. They brandish their sticks, run and yell, dart to and fro, like young Indians. They rob bird's nests, steal the eggs, pierce them and blow them. They capture the young birds, and are not above killing the parents that fly frantically to the rescue.

I knew of boys who ground captured birds to death on a grindstone. Who has not seen a boy fling stones at a helpless hop-toad?

As boys grow older to the age of reading they select, or at least love best, those stories of bloodshed and violence. Stevenson wrote that boys read for some element of the brute instinct in them. His two wonderful books *Treasure Island* and *Kidnapped* are full of fight and the killing of men. *Robinson Crusoe* is the only great boy's book I ever read that did not owe its charm to fighting. But still did not old Crusoe fight to live on his lonely island? And this wonderful tale is full of hunting, and has at the end the battle with cannibals.

When lads grow up they become hunters, almost without exception, at least in spirit if not in deed. Early days and environment decide whether or not a man becomes a hunter. In all my life I have met only two grown men who did not care to go prowling and hunting in the woods with a gun. An exception proves a great deal, but all the same most men, whether they have a chance or not, love to hunt. Hunters, therefore, there are of many degrees. Hunters of the lowly cotton-tail and the woodland squirrel; hunters of quail, woodcock, and grouse; hunters of wild ducks and geese; hunters of foxes—the red-coated English and the homespun clad American; hunters—which is a kinder name for trappers—of beaver, marten, otter, mink, all the furred animals;, hunters of deer, cat, wolf, bear, antelope, elk, moose, caribou; hunters of the barren lands where the ice is king and where there are polar bears, white foxes, musk-ox, walrus. Hunters of different animals of different countries. African hunters for lion, rhinoceros, elephant, buffalo, eland, hartebeest, giraffe, and a hundred species made known to all the world by such classical sportsmen as Selous, Roosevelt, Stewart Edward White.

But they are all hunters and their game is the deadly chase in the open or the wild. There are hunters who hate action, who hate to walk and climb and toil and wear themselves out to get a shot. Such men are hunters still, but still not men! There are hunters who have game driven up to them. I heard a story told by an officer whom I believe. In the early days of

the war he found himself somewhere on the border between
Austria and Germany. He was invited to a hunt by personages
of high degree. They motored to a sequestered palace in the
forest, and next day motored to a shooting-lodge. At daylight
he was called, and taken to the edge of a forest and stationed
in an open glade. His stand was an upholstered divan placed
high in the forks of a tree. His guide told him that pretty soon
a doe would come out of the forest. But he was not to shoot
it. In fifteen minutes a lame buck would come out. But he
was not to shoot that one either. In ten more minutes another
buck would come out, and this third deer he was to kill. My
informant told me this was all very seriously meant. The gun
given him was large enough in calibre to kill an elephant. He
walked up the steps to the comfortable divan and settled
himself to await events. The doe trotted out exactly on sched-
ule time. So did the lame buck. They came from the woods
and were not frightened. The third deer, a large buck, was a
few moments late—three minutes to be exact. According to
instructions the American killed this buck—a matter that took
some nerve he said, for the buck walked out like a cow. That
night a big supper was given in the guest's honor. He had to
eat certain parts of the buck he had killed, and drink flagons
of wine. This kind of hunting must be peculiarly German or
Austrian, and illustrates the peculiar hunting ways of men.

A celebrated bear hunter and guide of the northwest told
me that for twenty years he had been taking eastern ministers—
preachers of the gospel—on hunting trips into the wild. He
assured me that of all the bloody murderers—waders in gore,
as he expressed it—these teachers of the gospel were the
worst. The moment they got out into the wild they wanted to
kill, kill, kill. He averred their natures seemed utterly to
change.

In reading the books of hunters and in listening to their
talks at Camp-fire Club dinners I have always been struck
with the expression of what these hunters felt, what they
thought they got out of hunting. The change from city to the
open wilderness; the difference between noise, tumult, dirt,
foul air, and the silence, the quiet, the cleanness and purity;
the sweet breath of God's country as so many called it; the

beauty of forest and mountain; the wildness of ridge and valley; the wonder of wild animals in their native haunts; and the zest, the joy, the excitement, the magnificent thrill of the stalk and the chase. No one of them ever dwelt upon the kill! It was mentioned, as a result, an end, a consummation. How strange that hunters believed these were the attractions of the chase! They felt them, to be sure, in some degree, or they would not remember them. But they never realized that these sensations were only incidental to hunting.

Men take long rides, hundreds and thousands of miles, to hunt. They endure hardships, live in camps with absolute joy. They stalk through the forest, climb the craggy peaks, labor as giants in the building of the pyramids, all with a tight clutch on a deadly rifle. They are keen, intent, strained, quiveringly eager all with a tight clutch on a deadly rifle. If hunters think while on a stalk—which matter I doubt considerably—they think about the lay of the land, or the aspect of it, of the habits and possibilities of their quarry, of their labor and chances, and particularly of the vague unrealized sense of comfort, pleasure, satisfaction in the moment. Tight muscles, alert eyes, stealthy steps, stalk and run and crawl and climb, breathlessness, a hot close-pressed chest, thrill on thrill, and sheer bursting riot of nerve and vein—these are the ordinary sensations and actions of a hunter. No ascent too lofty—no descent too perilous for him then, if he is a man as well as a hunter!

Take the Brazilian hunter of the jungle. He is solitary. He is sufficient to himself. He is a survival of the fittest. The number of his tribe are few. Nature sees to that. But he must eat, and therefore he hunts. He spears fish and he kills birds and beasts with a blow-gun. He hunts to live. But the manner of his action, though more skilful, is the same as any hunter's. Likewise his sensations, perhaps more vivid because hunting for him is a matter of life or death. Take the Gaucho of Patagonia—the silent lonely Indian hunter of the Pampas. He hunts with a *bola,* a thin thong or string at each end of which is a heavy leather-covered ball of stone or iron. This the Gaucho hurls through the air at the neck or legs of his quarry. The balls fly round—the thong binds tight—it is a deadly weapon. The user of it rides and stalks and sees and throws and feels the same as any other hunter. Time and place, weapon and game have little to do with any differences in hunters.

Up to this 1919 hunting trip in the wilds I had always marveled at the fact that naturalists and biologists hate sportsmen. Not hunters like the Yellow Knife Indians, or the snake-eating Bushmen of Australia, or the Terradel-Fuegians, or even the native country rabbit-hunters—but the so-called sportsmen. Naturalists and biologists have simply learned the truth why men hunt, and that when it is done in the name of sport, or for sensation, it is a degenerate business. Stevenson wrote beautiful words about "the hunter home from the hill," but so far as I can find out he never killed anything himself. He was concerned with the romance of the thought, with alliteration, and the singular charm of the truth—sunset and the end of the day, the hunter's plod down the hill to the cottage, to the home where wife and children awaited him. Indeed it is a beautiful truth, and not altogether in the past, for there are still farmers and pioneers.

Hunting is a savage primordial instinct inherited from our ancestors. It goes back through all the ages of man, and farther still—to the age when man was not man, but hairy ape, or some other beast from which we are descended. To kill is in the very marrow of our bones. If man after he developed into human state had taken to vegetable diet—which he never did take—he yet would have inherited the flesh-eating instincts of his animal forebears. And no instinct is ever wholly eradicated. But man was a meat eater. By brute strength, by sagacity, by endurance he killed in order to get the means of subsistence. If he did not kill he starved. And it is a matter of record, even down to modern times, that man has existed by cannibalism.

The cave-man stalked from his hole under a cliff, boldly forth with his huge club or stone mace. Perhaps he stole his neighbor's woman, but if so he had more reason to hunt than before—he had to feed her as well as himself. This cave-man, savagely descended, savagely surrounded, must have had to hunt all the daylight hours and surely had to fight to kill his food, or to keep it after he killed it. Long, long ages was the being called caveman in developing; more long ages he lived on the earth, in that dim dark mystic past; and just as long were his descendants growing into another and higher type of barbarian. But they and their children and grandchildren, and all their successive, innumerable, and varying descendants had to hunt meat and eat meat to live.

The brain of barbarian man was small, as shown by the size and shape of his skull, but there is no reason to believe its construction and use were any different from the use of other organs—the eye to see with—the ear to hear with—the palate to taste with. Whatever the brain of primitive man was it held at birth unlimited and innumerable instincts like those of its progenitors; and round and smooth in babyhood, as it was, it surely gathered its sensations, one after another in separate and habitual channels, until when manhood arrived it had its convolutions, its folds and wrinkles. And if instinct and tendency were born in the brain how truly must they be a part of bone, tissue, blood.

We cannot escape our inheritance. Civilization is merely a veneer, a thin-skinned polish over the savage and crude nature. Fear, anger, lust, the three great primal instincts are restrained, but they live powerfully in the breast of man. Self preservation is the first law of human life, and is included in fear. Fear of death is the first instinct. Then if for thousands, perhaps millions of years, man had to hunt because of his fear of death, had to kill meat to suvive—consider the ineradicable and permanent nature of the instinct.

The secret now of the instinctive joy and thrill and wildness of the chase lies clear.

Stealing through the forest or along the mountain slope, eyes roving, ears sensitive to all vibrations of the air, nose as keen as that of a hound, hands tight on a deadly rifle, we unconsciously go back. We go back to the primitive, to the savage state of man. Therein lies the joy. How sweet, vague, unreal those sensations of strange familiarity with wild places we know we never saw before! But a million years before that hour a hairy ancestor of ours felt the same way in the same kind of a place, and in us that instinct survives. That is the secret of the wonderful strange charm of wild places, of the barren rocks of the desert wilderness, of the great-walled lonely canyons. Something now in our blood, in our bones once danced in men who lived then in similar places. And lived by hunting!

The child is father to the man. In the light of this instinct how easy to understand his boyish cruelty. He is true to nature. Unlimited and infinite in his imagination when he hunts—whether with his toys or with real weapons. If he flings a stone and kills a toad he is instinctively killing meat for his home in the cave. How little difference between the lad and the man! For a man the most poignantly exciting, the most thrillingly wild is the chase when he is weaponless, when he runs and kills his quarry with a club. Here we have the essence of the matter. The hunter is proudest of his achievement in which he has not had the help of deadly weapons. Unconsciously he will brag and glow over that conquest wherein lay greatest peril to him—when he had nothing but his naked hands. What a hot gush of blood bursts over him! He goes back to his barbarian state when a man only felt. The savage lived in his sensations. He saw, heard, smelled, tasted, touched, but seldom thought. The earthy, the elemental of eye and ear and skin surrounded him. When the man goes into the wilderess to change into a hunter that surviving kinship with the savage revives in his being, and all unconsciously dominates him with driving passion. Passion it is because for long he has been restrained in the public haunts of men. His real nature has been hidden. The hunting of game inhibits his thoughts. He feels only. He forgets himself. He sees the track, he hears the stealthy step, he smells the wild scent; and his blood dances with the dance of the ages. Then he is a killer. Then the ages roll back. Then he is brother to the savage. Then all unconsciously he lives the chase, the fight, the death-dealing moment as they were lived by all his ancestors down through the misty past.

What then should be the attitude of a thoughtful man toward this liberation of an instinct—that is to say, toward the game or sport or habit of hunting to kill?

Not easily could I decide this for myself. After all life is a battle. Eternally we are compelled to fight. If we do not fight, if we do not keep our bodies strong, supple, healthy, soon we succumb to some germ or other that gets a hold in our blood or lungs and fights for its life, its species, until it kills us. Fight therefore is absolutely necessary to long life, and Alas! eventually that fight must be lost. The savages, the Babylonians, the Persians, the Greeks all worshipped physical prowess in man. Manhood, strength—the symbols of fight! To be physically strong and well a man must work hard, with frequent intervals of change of exercise, and he must eat meat. I am not a great meat eater, but I doubt if I could do much physical labor or any brain work on a vegetable diet. Therefore I hold it fair and manly to go once a year to the wilderess to hunt. Let that hunt be clean hard toil, as hard as I can stand! Perhaps nature created the lower animals for the use of man. If I had been the creator I think I would have made it possible for the so-called higher animal man to live on air.

Somewhere I read a strange remarkable story about monkeys and priests in the jungle of India. An old order of priests had from time out of mind sent two of their comrades into the jungle to live with the monkeys, to tame them, feed them, study them, love them. And these priests told an incredible story, yet one that haunted with its possibilities of truth. After a long term of years in which one certain priest had lived with the monkeys and they had learned truly he meant them no harm and only loved them, at rare moments an old monkey would come to him and weep and weep in the most terrible and tragic manner. This monkey wanted to tell something, but could not speak. But the priest knew that the monkey was trying to tell him how once the monkey people had been human like him. Only they had retrograded in the strange scale of evolution. And the terrible weeping was for loss— loss of physical stature, of speech, perhaps of soul.

What a profound and stunning idea! Does evolution work backward? Could nature in its relentless inscrutable design for the unattainable perfection have developed man only to start him backward toward the dim ages whence he sprang? Who knows! But every man can love wild animals. Every man can study and try to understand the intelligence of his horse, the loyalty of his dog. And every hunter can hunt less with his instinct, and more with an understanding of his needs, and a consideration for the beasts only the creator knows.

X

The last day of everything always comes. Time, like the tide, waits for no man. Anticipation is beautiful, but it is best and happiest to enjoy the present. Live while we may!

On this last day of my hunt we were up almost before it was light enough to see. The morning star shone radiant in the dark gray sky. All the other stars seemed dimmed by its glory. Silent as a grave was the forest. I started a fire, chopped wood so vigorously that I awakened Nielsen who came forth like a burly cave-man; and I washed hands and face in the icy cold brook. By the time breakfast was over the gold of the rising sun was tipping the highest pines on the ridges.

We started on foot, leaving the horses hobbled near camp. All the hounds appeared fit. Even Old Dan trotted along friskily. Pyle, a neighbor of Haught's, had come to take a hunt with us, bringing two dogs with him. For this last day I had formulated a plan. Edd and one of the boys were to take the hounds down on the east side of the great ridge that made the eastern wall of Dude Canyon. R. C. was to climb out on this ridge, and take his position at the most advantageous point. We had already chased half a dozen bears over this saddle, one of which was the big frosty-coated grizzly that Edd and Nielsen had shot at. The rest of us hurried to the head of Dude Canyon. Copple and I were to go down to the first promontories under the rim. The others were to await developments and go where Haught thought best to send them.

Copple and I started down over and around the crags, going carefully until we reached the open slope under the rim-rock. It seemed this morning that I was fresh, eager, agile like a goat on my feet. In my consciousness of this I boasted to Copple that I would dislodge fewer stones and so make less noise than he. The canyon sloped at an angle of about forty-five degrees, and we slid, stepped, jumped and ran down without starting an avalanche.

When we descended to the first bare cape of projecting rock the hour was the earliest in which I had been down under the rim. All the canyon and the great green gulf below were unusually fresh and beautiful. I heard the lonely call of strange birds and the low murmur of running water. An eagle soared in the sunlight. High above us to the east rose the magnificent slope of Dude Canyon. I gazed up to the black and green and silver ascent, up to the gold-tipped craggy crest where R. C. had his stand. I knew he could see me, but I could not see him. Afterward he told me that my red cap shone clearly out of green and gray, so he had no dfficulty in keeping track of my whereabouts. The thickets of aspens and oaks seemed now to stand on end. How dark in the shade and steely and cold they looked! That giant ridge still obstructed the sun, and all on this side of it, under its frowning crest and slope was dark and fresh and cool in shadow. The ravines were choked black with spruce trees. Here along this gray shady slant of wall, in niches and cracks, and under ledges, and on benches, were the beds of the bears. Even as I gazed momentarily I expected to see a bear. It looked two hundred yards across the canyon from where we stood, but Copple declared it was a thousand. On our other side capes and benches and groves were bright in sunshine, clear across the rough breaks to the west wall of Dude Canyon. I saw a flock of wild pigeons below. Way out and beyond rolled the floor of the basin, green and vast, like a ridged sea of pines, to the bold black Mazatzals so hauntingly beckoning from the distance. Copple spoke now and then, but I wanted to be silent. How wild and wonderful this place in the early morning!

But I had not long to meditate and revel in beauty and wildness. Far down across the mouth of the canyon, at the extreme southern end of that vast oak thicket, the hounds gave tongue. Old Dan first! In the still cool air how his great wolf-bay rang out the wildness of the time and place! Already Edd and Pyle had rounded the end of the east ridge and were coming up along the slope of Dude Canyon.

"Hounds workin' round," declared Copple. "Now I'll tell

you what. Last night a bear was feedin' along that end of the thicket. The hounds are millin' round tryin' to straighten out his trail . . . It's a dead cinch they'll jump a bear an' we'll see him.''

"Look everywhere!" I cautioned Copple, and my eyes roved and strained over all that vast slope. Suddenly I espied the flash of something black, far down the thicket, and tried to show it to my comrade.

"Let's go around an' down to that lower point of rock. It's a better stand than this. Closer to the thicket an' commands those. . . . By Golly, I see what you see! That's a bear, slippin' down. Stay with me now!''

Staying with Copple was a matter of utter disregard of clothes, limbs, life. He plunged off that bare ledge, slid flat on his back, and wormed feet first under manzanita, and gaining open slope got up to run and jump into another thicket. By staying with him I saw that I would have a way opened through the brush, and something to fall upon if I fell. He rimmed the edge of a deep gorge that made me dizzy. He leaped cracks. He let himself down over a ledge by holding to bushes. He found steps to descend little bluffs, and he flew across the open slides of weathered rock. I was afraid this short cut to the lower projecting cape of rock would end suddenly on some impassable break or cliff, but though the travel grew rough we still kept on. I wore only boots, trousers, and shirt, and cap, with cartridge belt strapped tight around me. It was a wonder I was not stripped. Some of my rags went to decorate the wake we left down that succession of ledges. But we made it, with me at least, bruised and ragged, dusty and choked, and absolutely breathless. My body burned as with fire. Hot sweat ran in streams down my chest. At last we reached the bare flat projecting cape of rock, and indeed it afforded an exceedingly favorable outlook. I had to sink down on the rock; I could not talk until I got my breath; but I used my eyes to every advantage. Neither Copple nor I could locate the black moving object we had seen from above. We were much closer to the hounds, though they still were baying a tangled cross trail. Fortunate it was for me that I was given these few moments to rest from my tremendous exertions.

My eyes searched the leaf-covered slope so brown and sear, and the shaggy thickets, and tried to pierce the black tangle of spruce patches. All at once, magically it seemed, my gaze held to a dark shadow, a bit of dense shade, under a large spruce tree. Something moved. Then a big bear rose right out of his bed of leaves, majestically as if disturbed, and turned his head back toward the direction of the baying hounds. Next he walked out. He stopped. I was quivering with eagerness to tell Copple, but I waited. Then the bear walked behind a tree and peeped out, only his head showing. After a moment again he walked out.

"Ben, aren't you ever going to see him?" I cried at last.

"What?" ejaculated Copple, in surprise.

"Bear!" and I pointed. "This side of dead spruce."

"No! . . . Reckon you see a stump . . . By Golly! I see him. He's a dandy. Reddish color . . . Doc, he's one of them mean old cinnamons."

"Watch! What will he do?—Ben, he hears the hounds."

How singularly thrilling to see him, how slowly he walked, how devoid of fear, how stately!

"Sure he hears them. See him look back. The son-of-a-gun! I'll bet he's given us the bear-laugh more than once."

"Ben, how far away is he?" I asked.

"Oh, that's eight hundred yards," declared Copple. "A long shot. Let's wait. He may work down closer. But most likely he'll run up-hill."

"If he climbs he'll go right to R. C.'s stand," I said, gazing upward.

"Sure will. There's no other saddle."

Then I decided that I would not shoot at him unless he started down. My excitement was difficult to control. I found it impossible to attend to my sensations, to think about what I was feeling. But the moment was full of suspense. The bear went into a small clump of spruces and stayed there a little while. Tantalizing moments! The hounds were hot upon his trail, still working to and fro in the oak thicket. I judged scarcely a mile separated them from the bear. Again he disappeared behind a little bush. Remembering that five pairs of sharp eyes could see me from the points above I stood up

and waved my red cap. I waved it wildly as a man waves a
red flag in moments of danger. Afterward R. C. said he saw
me plainly and understood my action. Again the bear had
showed, this time on an open slide, where he had halted. He
was looking across the canyon while I waved my cap.

"Ben, could he see us so far?" I asked.

"By Golly, I'll bet he does see us. You get to smokin' him
up. An' if you hit him don't be nervous if he starts for us.
Cinnamons are bad customers. Lay out five extra shells an'
make up your mind to kill him."

I dropped upon one knee. The bear started down, coming
towards us over an open slide. "Aim a little coarse an' follow
him," said Copple. I did so, and tightening all my muscles
into a ball, holding my breath, I fired. The bear gave a savage
kick backwards. He jerked back to bite at his haunch. A
growl, low, angry, vicious followed the echoes of my rifle.
Then it seemed he pointed his head toward us and began to
run down the slope, looking our way all the time.

"By Golly!" yelled Copple. "You stung him one an' he's
comin'! . . . Now you've got to shoot some. He can roll
down-hill an' run up-hill like a jack rabbit. Take your time—
wait for open shots—an' make sure!"

Copple's advice brought home to me what could happen
even with the advantage on my side. Also it brought the cold
tight prickle to my skin, the shudder that was not a thrill, the
pressure of blood running too swiftly. I did not feel myself
shake, but the rifle was unsteady. I rested an elbow on my
knee, yet still I had difficulty in keeping the sight on him. I
could get it on him, but could not keep it there. Again he
came out into the open, at the head of a yellow slide, that
reached to a thicket below. I must not hurry, yet I had to
hurry. After all he had not so far to come and most of the
distance was under cover. Through my mind flashed Haught's
story of a cinnamon that kept coming with ten bullets in him.

"Doc, he's paddin' along!" warned Copple. " Smoke some
of them shells!"

Straining every nerve I aimed as before, only a little in
advance, held tight and pulled at the same instant. The bear
doubled up in a ball and began to roll down the slide. He

scattered the leaves. Then into the thicket he crashed, knocking the oaks, and cracking the brush.

"Some shot!" yelled Copple. "He's your bear!"

But my bear continued to crash through the brush. I shot again and yet again, missing both times. Apparently he was coming, faster now—and then he showed dark almost at the foot of our slope. Trees were thick there. I could not see there, and I could not look for bear and reload at the same moment. My fingers were not very nimble.

"Don't shoot," shouted Copple. "He's your bear. I never make any mistakes when I see game hit."

"But I see him coming!"

"Where? . . . By Golly! that's another bear. He's black. Yours is red. . . . Look sharp. Next time he shows smoke him!"

I saw a flash of black across an open space—I heard a scattering of gravel. But I had no chance to shoot. Then both of us heard a bear running in thick leaves.

"He's gone down the canyon," said Copple. "Now look for your bear."

"Listen Ben. The hounds are coming fast. There's Rock. —There's Sue."

"I see them. Old Dan—what do you think of that old dog? . . . There!—your red bear's still comin' . . . He's bad hurt."

Though Copple tried hard to show me where, and I strained my eyes, I could not see the bear. I could not locate the threshing of brush. I knew it seemed close enough for me to be glad I was not down in that thicket. How the hounds made the welkin ring! Rock was in the lead. Sue was next. And Old Dan must have found the speed of his best days. Strange he did not bay all down that slope! When Rock and Sue headed the bear then I saw him. He sat up on his haunches ready to fight, but they did not attack him. Instead they began to yelp wildly. I dared not shoot again for fear of hitting one of them. Old Dan just beat the rest of the pack to the bear. Up pealed a yelping chorus. I had never heard Old Dan bay a bear at close range. With deep, hoarse, quick, wild roars he dominated that medley. A box canyon took up the bays, cracking them back in echo from wall to wall.

From the saddle of the great ridge above pealed down R. C.'s: "Waahoo!"

I saw him silhouetted dark against the sky line. He waved and I answered. Then he disappeared.

Nielsen bellowed from the craggy cape above and behind us. From down the canyon Edd sent up his piercing: "Ki Yi!" Then Takahashi appeared opposite to us, like a goat on a promontory. How his: "Banzai!" rang above the baying of the hounds!

"We'd better hurry down an' across," said Copple. "Reckon the hounds will jump that bear or some one else will get there first. We got to skedaddle!"

As before we fell into a manzanita thicket and had to crawl. Then we came out upon the rim of a box canyon where the echoes made such a din. It was too steep to descend. We had to head it, and Copple took chances. Loose boulders tripped me and stout bushes saved me. We knocked streams of rock and gravel down into this gorge, sending up a roar as of falling water. But we got around. A steep slope lay below, all pine needles and leaves. From this point I saw Edd on the opposite slope.

"I stopped one bear," I yelled. "Hurry. Look out for the dogs!"

Then, imitating Copple, I sat down and slid as on a toboggan for some thirty thrilling yards. Some of my anatomy and more of my rags I left behind me. But it was too exciting then to think of hurts. I managed to protect at least my rifle. Copple was charging into the thicket below. I followed him into the dark gorge, where huge boulders lay, and a swift brook ran, and leaves two feet deep carpeted the shady canyon bed. It was gloomy down into the lower part. I saw where bear had turned over the leaves making a dark track.

"The hounds have quit," called Copple suddenly. "I told you he was your bear."

We yelled. Somebody above us answered. Then we climbed up the opposite slope, through a dense thicket, crossing a fresh bear track, a running track, and soon came into an open rocky slide where my bear lay surrounded by the hounds, with Old Dan on guard. The bear was red in color, with silky fur, a long keen head, and fine limbs, and of goodly size.

"Cinnamon," declared Copple, and turning him over he pointed to a white spot on his breast. "Fine bear. About four hundred pounds. Maybe not so heavy. But he'll take some packin' up to the rim!"

Then I became aware of the other men. Takahashi had arrived on the scene first, finding the bear dead. Edd came next, and after him Pyle.

I sat down for a much needed rest. Copple interested himself in examining the bear, finding that my first shot had hit him in the flank, and my second had gone through the middle of his body. Next Copple amused himself by taking pictures of bear and hounds. Old Dan came to me and lay beside me, and looked as if to say: "Well, we got him!"

Yells from both sides of the canyon were answered by Edd. R. C. was rolling the rocks on his side at a great rate. But Nielsen on the other side beat him to us. The Norwegian crashed the brush, sent the avalanches roaring, and eventually reached us, all dirty, ragged, bloody, with fire in his eye. He had come all the way from the rim in short order. What a performance that must have been! He said he thought he might be needed. R. C. guided by Edd's yells, came cracking the brush down to us. Pale he was and wet with sweat, and there were black brush marks across his face. His eyes were keen and sharp. He had started down for the same reason as Nielsen's. But he had to descend a slope so steep that he had to hold on to keep from sliding down. And he had jumped a big bear out of a bed of leaves. The bed was still warm. R. C. said he had smelled bear, and that his toboggan slide down that slope, with bears all around for all he knew, had started the cold sweat on him.

Presently George Haught joined us, having come down the bed of the canyon.

"We knew you'd got a bear," said George. "Father heard the first two bullets hit meat. An' I heard him rollin' down the slope."

"Well!" exclaimed R. C. "That's what made those first two shots sound so strange to me. Different from the last two. Sounded like soft dead pats! And it was lead hitting flesh. I heard it half a mile away!"

This matter of the sound of bullets hitting flesh and being heard at a great distance seemed to me the most remarkable feature of our hunt. Later I asked Haught. He said he heard my first two bullets strike and believed from the peculiar sound that I had my bear. And his stand was fully a mile away. But the morning was unusually still and sound carried far.

The men hung my bear from the forks of a maple. Then they decided to give us time to climb up to our stands before putting the hounds on the other fresh trail.

Nielsen, R. C., and I started to climb back up to the points. Only plenty of time made it possible to scale those rugged bluffs. Nielsen distanced us, and eventually we became separated. The sun grew warm. The bees hummed. After a while we heard the baying of the hounds. They were working westward under the bases of the bluffs. We rimmed the heads of several gorges, climbed and crossed the west ridge of Dude Canyon, and lost the hounds somewhere as we traveled.

R. C. did not seem to mind this misfortune any more than I. We were content. Resting a while we chose the most accessible ridge and started the long climb to the rim. Westward under us opened a great noble canyon full of forests, thicketed slopes, cliffs and caves and crags. Next time we rested we again heard the hounds, far away at first, but gradually drawing closer. In half an hour they appeared right under us again. Their baying, however, grew desultory, and lacked the stirring note. Finally we heard Edd calling and whistling to them. After that for a while all was still. Then pealed up the clear tuneful melody of Edd's horn, calling off the chase for that day and season.

"All over," said R. C. "Are you glad?"

"For Old Dan's sake and Tom's and the bears—yes," I replied.

"Me, too! But I'd never get enough of this country."

We proceeded on our ascent over and up the broken masses of rock, climbing slowly and easily, making frequent and long rests. We liked to linger in the sun on the warm piny mossy benches. Every shady cedar or juniper wooed us to tarry a moment. Old bear tracks and fresh deer tracks held the same interest, though our hunt was over. Above us the gray broken mass of rim towered and loomed, more formidable as we neared it. Sometimes we talked a little, but mostly we were silent.

Like an Indian, at every pause, I gazed out into the void. How sweeping and grand the long sloping lines of ridges from the rim down! Away in the east ragged spurs of peaks showed hazily, like uncertain mountains on the desert. South ranged the upheaved and wild Mazatzals. Everywhere beneath me, for leagues and leagues extended the timbered hills of green, the gray outcroppings of rocks, the red bluffs, the golden patches of grassy valleys, lost in the canyons. All these swept away in a vast billowy ocean of wilderness to become dim in the purple of distance. And the sun was setting in a blaze of gold. From the rim I took a last lingering look and did not marvel that I loved this wonderland of Arizona.

CHAPTER TWO

Death Valley

Of the five hundred and fifty-seven thousand square miles of desert-land in the southwest Death Valley is the lowest below sea level, the most arid and desolate. It derives its felicitous name from the earliest days of the gold strike in California, when a caravan of Mormons, numbering about seventy, struck out from Salt Lake, to cross the Mojave Desert and make a short cut to the gold fields. All but two of these prospectors perished in the deep, iron-walled, ghastly sink-holes, which from that time became known as Death Valley.

The survivors of this fatal expedition brought news to the world that the sombre valley of death was a treasure mine of minerals; and since then hundreds of prospectors and wanderers have lost their lives there. To seek gold and to live in the lonely waste places of the earth have been and ever will be driving passions of men.

My companion on this trip was a Norwegian named Nielsen. On most of my trips to lonely and wild places I have been fortunate as to comrades or guides. The circumstances of my meeting Nielsen were so singular that I think they will serve as an interesting introduction. Some years ago I received a letter, brief, clear and well-written, in which the writer stated that he had been a wanderer over the world, a sailor before the mast, and was now a prospector for gold. He had taken four trips alone down into the desert of Sonora, and in many other places of the southwest, and knew the prospecting game. Somewhere he had run across my story *Desert Gold* in which I told about a lost gold mine. And the point of his letter was that if I could give him some idea as to where the lost gold mine was located he would go find it and give me half. His name was Sievert Nielsen. I wrote him that to my regret the lost gold mine existed only in my imagination, but if he would come to Avalon to see me perhaps we might both profit by such a meeting. To my surprise he came. He was a man of about thirty-five, of magnificent physique, weighing about one hundred and ninety, and he was so enormously broad across the shoulders that he did not look his five feet ten. He had a wonderful head, huge, round, solid, like a cannonball. And his bronzed face, his regular features, square firm jaw, and clear gray eyes, fearless and direct, were singularly attractive to me. Well educated, with a strange calm poise, and a cool courtesy, not common in Americans, he evidently was a man of good family, by his own choice a rolling stone and adventurer.

Nielsen accompanied me on two trips into the wilderness of Arizona, on one of which he saved my life, and on the other he rescued all our party from a most uncomfortable and possibly hazardous situation—but these are tales I may tell elsewhere. In January 1919 Nielsen and I traveled around the desert of southern California from Palm Springs to Picacho, and in March we went to Death Valley.

Nowadays a little railroad, the Tonapah and Tidewater Railroad, runs northward from the Santa Fe over the barren Mojave, and it passes within fifty miles of Death Valley.

It was sunset when we arrived at Death Valley Junction—a weird, strange sunset in drooping curtains of transparent cloud, lighting up dark mountain ranges, some peaks of which were clear-cut and black against the sky, and others veiled in trailing storms, and still others white with snow. That night in the dingy little store I heard prospectors talk about float, which meant gold on the surface, and about high grade ores, zinc, copper, silver, lead, manganese, and about how borax was mined thirty years ago, and hauled out of Death Valley by teams of twenty mules. Next morning, while Nielsen packed the outfit, I visited the borax mill. It was the property of an English firm, and the work of hauling, grinding, roasting borax ore went on day and night. Inside it was as dusty and full of a powdery atmosphere as an old-fashioned flour mill. The ore was hauled by train from some twenty miles over toward the valley, and was dumped from a high trestle into shutes that fed the grinders. For an hour I watched this constant stream of borax as it slid down into the hungry crushers, and I listened to the chalk-faced operator who yelled in my ear. Once he picked a piece of gypsum out of the borax. He said the mill was getting out twenty-five hundred sacks a day. The most significant thing he said was that men did not last long at such labor, and in the mines six months appeared to be the limit of human endurance. How soon I had enough of that choking air in the room where the borax was ground! And the place where the borax was roasted in huge round revolving furnaces—I found that intolerable. When I got out into the cool clean desert air I felt an immeasurable relief. And that relief made me thoughtful of the lives of men who labored, who were chained by necessity, by duty or habit, or by love, to the hard tasks of the world. It did not seem fair. These laborers of the borax mines and mills, like the stokers of ships, and coal-diggers, and blast-furnace hands—like thousands and millions of men, killed themselves outright or impaired their strength, and when they were gone or rendered useless others were found to take their places. Whenever I come in contact with some phase of this problem of life I take the meaning or the lesson of it to myself. And as the years go by my respect and reverence and wonder increase for these men of elemental lives, these horny-handed toilers with physical things, these uncomplaining users of brawn and bone, these giants who breast the elements, who till the earth and handle iron, who fight the natural forces with their bodies.

That day about noon I looked back down the long gravel and greasewood slope which we had ascended and I saw the borax-mill now only a smoky blot on the desert floor. When we reached the pass between the Black Mountains and the Funeral Mountains we left the road, and were soon lost to the works of man. How strange a gladness, a relief! Something dropped away from me. I felt the same subtle change in Nielsen. For one thing he stopped talking, except an occasional word to the mules.

The blunt end of the Funeral Range was as remarkable as its name. It sheered up very high, a saw-toothed range with colored strata tilted at an angle of forty-five degrees. Zigzag veins of black and red and yellow, rather dull, ran through the great drab-gray mass. This end of the range, an iron mountain, frowned down upon us with hard and formidable aspect. The peak was draped in streaky veils of rain from low-dropping clouds that appeared to have lodged there. All below lay clear and cold in the sunlight.

Our direction lay to the westward, and at that altitude, about three thousand feet, how pleasant to face the sun! For the wind was cold. The narrow shallow wash leading down from the pass deepened, widened, almost imperceptibly at first, and then gradually until its proportions were striking. It was a gully where the gravel washed down during rains, and where a scant vegetation, greasewood, and few low cacti and scrubby sage struggled for existence. Not a bird or lizard or living creature in sight! The trail was getting lonely. From time to time I looked back, because as we could not see far ahead all the superb scene spread and towered behind us. By and bye our wash grew to be a wide canyon, winding away from under the massive, impondering wall of the Funeral Range. The high side of this magnificent and impressive line of mountains faced west—a succession of unscalable slopes of bare ragged rock, jagged and jutted, dark drab, rusty iron, with gray and oblique strata running through them far as eye could see. Clouds soared around the peaks. Shadows sailed along the slopes.

Walking in loose gravel was as hard as trudging along in sand. After about fifteen miles I began to have leaden feet. I did not mind hard work, but I wanted to avoid over-exertion. When I am extremely wearied my feelings are liable to be colored somewhat by depression or melancholy. Then it always bothered me to get tired while Nielsen kept on with his wonderful stride.

"Say, Nielsen, do you take me for a Yaqui?" I complained. "Slow up a little."

Then he obliged me, and to cheer me up he told me about a little tramping experience he had in Baja California. Somewhere on the east slope of the Sierra Madre his burros strayed or were killed by mountain-lions, and he found it imperative to strike at once for the nearest ranch below the border, a distance of one hundred and fifty miles. He could carry only so much of his outfit, and as some of it was valuable to him he discarded all his food except a few biscuits, and a canteen of water. Resting only a few hours, without sleep at all, he walked the hundred and fifty miles in three days and nights. I believed that Nielsen, by telling me such incidents of his own wild experience, inspired me to more endurance than I knew I possessed.

As we traveled on down the canyon its dimensions continued to grow. It finally turned to the left, and opened out wide into a valley running west. A low range of hills faced us, rising in a long sweeping slant of earth, like the incline of a glacier, to rounded spurs. Half way up this slope, where the brown earth lightened there showed an outcropping of clay-amber and cream and cinnamon and green, all exquisitely vivid and clear. This bright spot appeared to be isolated. Far above it rose other clay slopes of variegated hues, red and russet and mauve and gray, and colors indescribably merged, all running in veins through this range of hills. We faced the west again, and descending this valley were soon greeted by a region of clay hills, bare, cone-shaped, fantastic in shade, slope, and ridge, with a high sharp peak dominating all. The colors were mauve, taupe, pearl-gray, all stained by a descending band of crimson, as if a higher slope had been stabbed to let its life blood flow down. The softness, the richness and beauty of this texture of earth amazed and delighted my eyes.

Quite unprepared, at time approaching sunset, we reached and rounded a sharp curve, to see down and far away, and to be held mute in our tracks. Between a white-mantled mountain range on the left and the dark-striped lofty range on the right I could see far down into a gulf, a hazy void, a vast stark valley that seemed streaked and ridged and canyoned, an abyss into which veils of rain were dropping and over which broken clouds hung, pierced by red and gold rays.

Death Valley! Far down and far away still, yet confounding at first sight! I gazed spellbound. It oppressed my heart. Nielsen stood like a statue, silent, absorbed for a moment, then he strode on. I followed, and every second saw more and different aspects, that could not, however, change the first stunning impression. Immense, unreal, weird! I went on down the widening canyon, looking into that changing void. How full of color! It smoked. The traceries of streams or shining white washes brightened the floor of the long dark pit. Patches and plains of white, borax flats or alkali, showed up like snow. A red haze, sinister and sombre, hung over the eastern ramparts of this valley, and over the western drooped gray veils of rain, like thinnest lacy clouds, through which gleams of the sun shone.

Nielsen plodded on, mindful of our mules. But I lingered, and at last checked my reluctant steps at an open high point with commanding and magnificent view. As I did not attempt the impossible—to write down thoughts and sensations— afterward I could remember only a few. How desolate and grand! The far-away, lonely and terrible places of the earth were the most beautiful and elevating. Life's little day seemed so easy to understand, so pitiful. As the sun began to set and the storm-clouds moved across it this wondrous scene darkened, changed every moment, brightened, grew full of luminous red light and then streaked by golden gleams. The tips of the Panamint Mountains came out silver above the purple clouds. At sunset the moment was glorious—dark, forbidding, dim, weird, dismal, yet still tinged with gold. Not like any other scene! Dante's Inferno! Valley of Shadows! Canyon of Purple Veils!

When the sun had set and all that upheaved and furrowed world of rock had received a mantle of gray, and a slumberous sulphurous ruddy haze slowly darkened to purple and black, then I realized more fully that I was looking down into Death Valley.

Twilight was stealing down when I caught up with Nielsen. He had selected for our camp a protected nook near where the canyon floor bore some patches of sage, the stalks and roots of which would serve for firewood. We unpacked, fed the mules some grain, pitched our little tent and made our bed all in short order. But it was dark long before we had supper. During the meal we talked a little, but afterward, when the chores were done, and the mules had become quiet, and the strange thick silence had settled down upon us, we did not talk at all.

The night was black, with sky mostly obscured by clouds. A pale haze marked the west where the after glow had faded; in the south one radiant star crowned a mountain peak. I strolled away in the darkness and sat down upon a stone. How intense the silence! Dead, vast, sepulchre-like, dreaming, waiting, a silence of ages, burdened with the history of the past, awful! I strained my ears for sound of insect or rustle of sage or drop of weathered rock. The soft cool desert wind was soundless. This silence had something terrifying in it, making me a man alone on the earth. The great spaces, the wild places as they had been millions of years before! I seemed to divine how through them man might develop from savage to a god, and how alas! he might go back again.

When I returned to camp Nielsen had gone to bed and the fire had burned low. I threw on some branches of sage. The fire blazed up. But it seemed different from other camp-fires. No cheer, no glow, no sparkle! Perhaps it was owing to scant and poor wood. Still I thought it was owing as much to the place. The sadness, the loneliness, the desolateness of this place weighed upon the camp-fire the same as it did upon my heart.

We got up at five-thirty. At dawn the sky was a cold leaden gray, with a dull gold and rose in the east. A hard wind, eager and nipping, blew up the canyon. At six o'clock the sky brightened somewhat and the day did not promise so threatening.

An hour later we broke camp. Traveling in the early morning was pleasant and we made good time down the winding canyon, arriving at Furnace Creek about noon, where we halted to rest. This stream of warm water flowed down from a gully that headed up in the Funeral Mountains. It had a disagreeable taste, somewhat acrid and soapy. A green thicket of brush was indeed welcome to the eye. It consisted of a

rank coarse kind of grass, and arrowweed, mesquite, and
tamarack. The last named bore a pink fuzzy blossom, not
unlike pussywillow, which was quite fragrant. Here the dead-
ness of the region seemed further enlivened by several small
birds, speckled and gray, two ravens, and a hawk. They all
appeared to be hunting food. On a ridge above Furnace Creek
we came upon a spring of poison water. It was clear, sparkling, with a greenish cast, and it deposited a white crust on
the margins. Nielsen, kicking around in the sand, unearthed a
skull, bleached and yellow, yet evidently not so very old.
Some thirsty wanderer had taken his last drink at that deceiving spring. The gruesome and the beautiful, the tragic and the
sublime, go hand in hand down the naked shingle of this
desolate desert.

While tramping around in the neighborhood of Furnace
Creek I happened upon an old almost obliterated trail. It led
toward the ridges of clay, and when I had climbed it a little
ways I began to get an impression that the slopes on the other
side must run down into a basin or canyon. So I climbed to
the top.

The magnificent scenes of desert and mountain, like the
splendid things of life, must be climbed for. In this instance I
was suddenly and stunningly confronted by a yellow gulf of
cone-shaped and fan-shaped ridges, all bare crinkly clay, of
gold, of amber, of pink, of bronze, of cream, all tapering
down to round-knobbed lower ridges, bleak and barren, yet
wonderfully beautiful in their stark purity of denudation; until
at last far down between two widely separated hills shone,
dim and blue and ghastly, with shining white streaks like
silver streams—the Valley of Death. Then beyond it climbed
the league-long red slope, merging into the iron-buttressed
base of the Panamint Range, and here line on line, and bulge
on bulge rose the bold benches, and on up the unscalable
outcroppings of rock, like colossal ribs of the earth, on and
up the steep slopes to where their density of blue black color
began to thin out with streaks of white, and thence upward to
the last noble height, where the cold pure snow gleamed
against the sky.

I descended into this yellow maze, this world of gullies and ridges where I found it difficult to keep from getting lost. I did lose my bearings, but as my boots made deep imprints in the soft clay I knew it would be easy to back-track my trail. After a while this labyrinthine series of channels and dunes opened into a wide space enclosed on three sides by denuded slopes, mostly yellow. These slopes were smooth, graceful, symmetrical, with tiny tracery of erosion, and each appeared to retain its own color, yellow or cinnamon or mauve. But they were always dominated by a higher one of a different color. And this mystic region sloped and slanted to a great amphitheater that was walled on the opposite side by a mountain of bare earth, of every hue, and of a thousand ribbed and scalloped surfaces. At its base the golds and russets and yellows were strongest, but ascending its slopes were changing colors—a dark beautiful mouse color on one side and a strange pearly cream on the other. Between these great corners of the curve climbed ridges of gray and heliotrope and amber, to meet wonderful veins of green—green as the sea in sunlight—and tracery of white—and on the bold face of this amphitheater, high up, stood out a zigzag belt of dull red, the stain of which had run down to tinge the other hues. Above all this wondrous coloration upheaved the bare breast of the mountain, growing darker with earthy browns, up to the gray old rock ramparts.

This place affected me so strangely, so irresistibly that I remained there a long time. Something terrible had happened there to men. I felt that. Something tragic was going on right then—the wearing down, the devastation of the old earth. How plainly that could be seen! Geologically it was more remarkable to me than the Grand Canyon. But it was the appalling meaning, the absolutely indescribable beauty that overcame me. I thought of those who had been inspiration to me in my work, and I suffered a pang that they could not be there to see and feel with me.

On my way out of this amphitheater a hard wind swooped down over the slopes, tearing up the colored dust in sheets and clouds. It seemed to me each gully had its mystic pall of color. I lost no time climbing out. What a hot choking ordeal! But I never would have missed it even had I known I would

get lost. Looking down again the scene was vastly changed.
A smoky weird murky hell with the dull sun gleaming magenta-
hued through the shifting pall of dust!

In the afternoon we proceeded leisurely, through an atmosphere growing warmer and denser, down to the valley,
reaching it at dusk. We followed the course of Furnace Creek
and made camp under some cottonwood trees, on the west
slope of the valley.

The wind blew a warm gale all night. I lay awake a while
and slept with very little covering. Toward dawn the gale died
away. I was up at five-thirty. The morning broke fine, clear,
balmy. A flare of pale gleaming light over the Funeral Range
heralded the sunrise. The tips of the higher snow-capped
Panamints were rose colored, and below them the slopes were
red. The bulk of the range showed dark. All these features
gradually brightened until the sun came up. How blazing and
intense! The wind began to blow again. Under the cotton-
woods with their rustling leaves, and green so soothing to the
eye, it was very pleasant.

Beyond our camp stood green and pink thickets of tamarack, and some dark velvety green alfalfa fields, made possible by the spreading of Furnace Creek over the valley slope.
A man lived there, and raised this alfalfa for the mules of the
borax miners. He lived there alone and his was indeed a
lonely, wonderful, and terrible life. At this season a few
Shoshone Indians were camped near, helping him in his
labors. This lone rancher's name was Denton, and he turned
out to be a brother of a Denton, hunter and guide, whom I
had met in Lower California.

Like all desert men, used to silence, Denton talked with
difficulty, but the content of his speech made up for its
brevity. He told us about the wanderers and prospectors he
had rescued from death by starvation and thirst; he told us
about the terrific noonday heat of summer; and about the
incredible and horrible midnight furnace gales that swept
down the valley. With the mercury at one hundred and twenty-
five degrees at midnight, below the level of the sea, when
these furnace blasts bore down upon him, it was just all he
could do to live. No man could spend many summers there.
As for white women—Death Valley was fatal to them. The

Indians spent the summers up on the mountains. Denton said heat affected men differently. Those who were meat eaters or alcohol drinkers, could not survive. Perfect heart and lungs were necessary to stand the heat and density of atmosphere below sea level. He told of a man who had visited his cabin, and had left early in the day, vigorous and strong. A few hours later he was found near the oasis unable to walk, crawling on his hands and knees, dragging a full canteen of water. He never knew what ailed him. It might have been heat, for the thermometer registered one hundred and thirty-five, and it might have been poison gas. Another man, young, of heavy and powerful build, lost seventy pounds weight in less than two days, and was nearly dead when found. The heat of Death Valley quickly dried up blood, tissue, bone. Denton told of a prospector who started out at dawn strong and rational, to return at sunset so crazy that he had to be tied to keep him out of the water. To have drunk his fill then would have killed him! He had to be fed water by spoonful. Another wanderer came staggering into the oasis, blind, with horrible face, and black swollen tongue protruding. He could not make a sound. He also had to be roped, as if he were a mad steer.

I met only one prospector during my stay in Death Valley. He camped with us. A rather undersized man he was, yet muscular, with brown wrinkled face and narrow dim eyes. He seemed to be smiling to himself most of the time. He liked to talk to his burros. He was exceedingly interesting. Once he nearly died of thirst, having gone from noon one day till next morning without water. He said he fell down often during this ordeal, but did not lose his senses. Finally the burros saved his life. This old fellow had been across Death Valley every month in the year. July was the worst. In that month crossing should not be attempted during the middle of the day.

I made the acquaintance of the Shoshone Indians, or rather through Nielsen I met them. Nielsen had a kindly, friendly way with Indians. There were half a dozen families, living in squalid tents. The braves worked in the fields for Denton and the squaws kept to the shade with their numerous children. They appeared to be poor. Certainly they were a ragged unpicturesque group. Nielsen and I visited them, taking an armload of canned fruit, and boxes of sweet crackers, which they received with evident joy. Through this overture I got a peep into one of the tents. The simplicity and frugality of the desert Piute or Navajo were here wanting. These children of the open wore white men's apparel and ate white men's food; and they even had a cook stove and a sewing machine in their tent. With all that they were trying to live like Indians. For me the spectacle was melancholy. Another manifestation added to my long list of degeneration of the Indians by the whites! The tent was a buzzing beehive of flies. I never before saw so many. In a corner I saw a naked Indian baby asleep on a goat skin, all his brown warm-tinted skin spotted black with flies.

Later in the day one of the Indian men called upon us at our camp. I was surprised to hear him use good English. He said he had been educated in a government school in California. From him I learned considerable about Death Valley. As he was about to depart, on the way to his labor in the fields, he put his hand in his ragged pocket and drew forth an old beaded hat band, and with calm dignity, worthy of any gift, he made me a present of it. Then he went on his way. The incident touched me. I had been kind. The Indian was not to be outdone. How that reminded me of the many instances of pride in Indians! Who yet has ever told the story of the Indian—the truth, the spirit, the soul of his tragedy?.

Nielsen and I climbed high up the west slope to the top of a gravel ridge swept clean and packed hard by the winds. Here I sat down while my companion tramped curiously around. At my feet I found a tiny flower, so tiny as to almost defy detection. The color resembled sage-gray and it had the fragrance of sage. Hard to find and wonderful to see—was its tiny blossom! The small leaves were perfectly formed, very soft, veined and scalloped, with a fine fuzz and a glistening sparkle. That desert flower of a day, in its isolation and fragility, yet its unquenchable spirit to live, was as great to me as the tremendous reddening bulk of the Funeral Moutains looming so sinisterly over me.

Then I saw some large bats with white heads flitting around in zigzag flights—assuredly new and strange creatures to me.

I had come up there to this high ridge to take advantage of the bleak lonely spot commanding a view of valley and mountains. Before I could compose myself to watch the valley I made the discovery that near me were six low gravelly mounds. Graves! One had two stones at head and foot. Another had no mark at all. The one nearest me had for the head a flat piece of board, with lettering so effaced by weather that I could not decipher the inscription. The bones of a horse lay littered about between the graves. What a lonely place for graves! Death Valley seemed to be one vast sepulchre. What had been the lives and deaths of these people buried here? Lonely, melancholy, nameless graves upon the windy desert slope!

By this time the long shadows had begun to fall. Sunset over Death Valley! A golden flare burned over the Panamints— long tapering notched mountains with all their rugged conformation showing. Above floated gold and gray and silver-edged clouds—below shone a whorl of dusky, ruddy bronze haze, gradually thickening. Dim veils of heat still rose from the pale desert valley. As I watched all before me seemed to change and be shrouded in purple. How bold and desolate a scene! What vast scale and tremendous dimension! The clouds paled, turned rosy for a moment with the afterglow, then deepened into purple gloom. A sombre smoky sunset, as if this Death Valley was the gateway of hell, and its sinister shades were upflung from fire.

The desert day was done and now the desert twilight descended. Twilight of hazy purple fell over the valley of shadows. The black bold lines of mountains ran across the sky and down into the valley and up on the other side. A buzzard sailed low in the foreground—fitting emblem of life in all that wilderness of suggested death. This fleeting hour was tranquil and sad. What little had it to do with the destiny of man! Death Valley was only a ragged rent of the old earth, from which men in their folly and passion, had sought to dig forth golden treasure. The air held a solemn stillness. Peace! How it rested my troubled soul! I felt that I was myself here, far different from my habitual self. Why had I longed to see Death Valley? What did I want of the desert that was naked, red, sinister, sombre, forbidding, ghastly, stark, dim and dark and dismal, the abode of silence and loneliness, the proof of death, decay, devastation and destruction, the majestic sublimity of desolation? The answer was that I sought the awful, the appalling and terrible because they harked me back to a primitive day where my blood and bones were bequeathed their heritage of the elements. That was the secret of the eternal fascination the desert exerted upon all men. It carried them back. It inhibited thought. It brought up the age-old sensations, so that I could feel, though I did not know it then, once again the all-satisfying state of the savage in nature.

When I returned to camp night had fallen. The evening star stood high in the pale sky, all alone and difficult to see, yet the more beautiful for that. The night appeared to be warmer or perhaps it was because no wind blew. Nielsen got supper, and ate most of it, for I was not hungry. As I sat by the camp-fire a flock of little bats, the smallest I had ever seen, darted from the wood-pile nearby and flew right in my face. They had no fear of man or fire. Their wings made a soft swishing sound. Later I heard the trill of frogs, which was the last sound I might have expected to hear in Death Valley. A sweet high-pitched melodious trill it reminded me of the music made by frogs in the Tamaulipas Jungle of Mexico. Every time I awakened that night, and it was often, I heard this trill. Once, too, sometime late, my listening ear caught faint mournful notes of a killdeer. How strange, and still sweeter than the trill! What a touch to the infinite silence and loneliness! A killdeer—bird of the swamps and marshes—what could he be doing in arid and barren Death Valley? Nature is mysterious and inscrutable.

Next morning the marvel of nature was exemplified even more strikingly. Out on the hard gravel-strewn slope I found some more tiny flowers of a day. One was a white daisy, very frail and delicate on long thin stem with scarcely any leaves. Another was a yellow flower, with four petals, a pale miniature California poppy. Still another was a purple-red flower, almost as large as a buttercup, with dark green leaves. Last and tiniest of all were infinitely fragile pink and white blossoms, on very flat plants, smiling wanly up from the desolate earth.

Nielsen and I made known to Denton our purpose to walk across the valley. He advised against it. Not that the heat was intense at this season, he explained, but there were other dangers, particularly the brittle salty crust of the sink-hole. Nevertheless we were not deterred from our purpose.

So with plenty of water in canteens and a few biscuits in our pockets we set out. I saw the heat veils rising from the valley floor, at that point one hundred and seventy-eight feet below sea level. The heat lifted in veils, like thin smoke. Denton had told us that in summer the heat came in currents, in waves. It blasted leaves, burned trees to death as well as men. Prospector watched for the leaden haze that thickened over the mountains, knowing then no man could dare the terrible sun. That day would be a hazed and glaring hell, leaden, copper, with sun blazing a sky of molten iron.

A long sandy slope of mesquite extended down to the bare crinkly floor of the valley, and here the descent to a lower level was scarcely perceptible. The walking was bad. Little mounds in the salty crust made it hard to place a foot on the level. This crust appeared fairly strong. But when it rang hollow under our boots, then I stepped very cautiously. The color was a dirty gray and yellow. Far ahead I could see a dazzling white plain that looked like frost or a frozen river. The atmosphere was deceptive, making this plain seem far away and then close at hand.

The excessively difficult walking and the thickness of the air tired me, so I plumped myself down to rest, and used my note-book as a means to conceal from the tireless Nielsen that I was fatigued. Always I found this a very efficient excuse, and for that matter it was profitable for me. I have forgotten more than I have ever written.

Rather overpowering, indeed, was it to sit on the floor of Death Valley, miles from the slopes that appeared so far away. It was flat, salty, alkali or borax ground, crusted and cracked. The glare hurt my eyes. I felt moist, hot, oppressed, in spite of a rather stiff wind. A dry odor pervaded the air, slightly like salty dust. Thin dust devils whirled on the bare flats. A valley-wide mirage shone clear as a mirror along the desert floor to the west, strange, deceiving, a thing both unreal and beautiful. The Panamints towered a wrinkled red grisly mass, broken by rough canyons, with long declines of talus like brown glaciers. Seamed and scarred! Indestructible by past ages, yet surely wearing to ruin! From this point I could not see the snow on the peaks. The whole mountain range seemed an immense red barrier of beetling rock. The Funeral Range was farther away and therefore more impressive. Its effect was stupendous. Leagues of brown chocolate slopes, scarred by slashes of yellow and cream, and shadowed black by sailing clouds, led up to the magnificently peaked and jutted summits.

Splendid as this was and reluctant as I felt to leave I soon joined Nielsen, and we proceeded onward. At last we reached the white winding plain, that had resembled a frozen river, and which from afar had looked so ghastly and stark. We found it to be a perfectly smooth stratum of salt glistening as if powdered. It was not solid, not stable. At pressure of a boot it shook like jelly. Under the white crust lay a yellow substance that was wet. Here appeared an obstacle we had not calculated upon. Nielsen ventured out on it and his feet sank in several inches. I did not like the wave of the crust. It resembled thin ice under a weight. Presently I ventured to take a few steps, and did not sink in so deeply or make such depression in the crust as Nielsen. We returned to the solid edge and deliberated. Nielsen said that by stepping quickly we could cross without any great risk, though it appeared reasonable that by standing still a person would sink into the substance.

"Well, Nielsen, you go ahead," I said, with an attempt at lightness. "You weigh one hundred and ninety. If you go through I'll turn back!"

Nielsen started with a laugh. The man courted peril. The bright face of danger must have been beautiful and alluring to him. I started after him—caught up with him—and stayed beside him. I could not have walked behind him over that strip of treacherous sink-hole. If I could have done so the whole adventure would have been meaningless to me. Nevertheless I was frightened. I felt the prickle of my skin, the stiffening of my hair, as well as the cold tingling thrills along my veins.

This place was the lowest point of the valley, in that particular location, and must have been upwards of two hundred feet below sea level. The lowest spot, called the Sink Hole, lay some miles distant, and was the terminus of this river of salty white.

We crossed it in safety. On the other side extended a long flat of upheaved crusts of salt and mud, full of holes and pitfalls, an exceedingly toilsome and painful place to travel, and for all we could tell, dangerous too. I had all I could do to watch my feet and find surfaces to hold my steps. Eventually we crossed this broken field, reaching the edge of the gravel slope, where we were very glad indeed to rest.

Denton had informed us that the distance was seven miles across the valley at the mouth of Furnace Creek. I had thought it seemed much less than that. But after I had toiled across it I was convinced that it was much more. It had taken us hours. How the time had sped! For this reason we did not tarry long on that side.

Facing the sun we found the return trip more formidable. Hot indeed it was—hot enough for me to imagine how terrible Death Valley would be in July or August. On all sides the mountains stood up dim and obscure and distant in haze. The heat veils lifted in ripples, and any object not near at hand seemed illusive. Nielsen set a pace for me on this return trip. I was quicker and surer of foot than he, but he had more endurance. I lost strength while he kept his unimpaired. So often he had to wait for me. Once when I broke through the crust he happened to be close at hand and quickly hauled me out. I got one foot wet with some acid fluid. We peered down into the murky hole. Nielsen quoted a prospector's saying: "Forty feet from hell!" That broken sharp crust of salt afforded the meanest traveling I had ever experienced. Slopes of weathered rock that slip and slide are bad; cacti, and especially choya cacti, are worse: the jagged and corrugated surfaces of lava are still more hazardous and painful. But this cracked floor of Death Valley, with its salt crusts standing on end, like pickets of a fence, beat any place for hard going that either Nielsen or I ever had encountered. I ruined my boots, skinned my shins, cut my hands. How those salt cuts stung!

We crossed the upheaved plain, then the strip of white, and reached the crinkly floor of yellow salt. The last hour taxed my endurance almost to the limit. When we reached the edge of the sand and the beginning of the slope I was hotter and thirstier than I had ever been in my life. It pleased me to see Nielsen wringing wet and panting. He drank a quart of water apparently in one gulp. And it was significant that I took the longest and deepest drink of water that I had ever had.

We reached camp at the end of this still hot summer day. Never had a camp seemed so welcome! What a wonderful thing it was to earn and appreciate and realize rest! The cottonwood leaves were rustling; bees were humming in the tamarack blossoms. I lay in the shade, resting my burning feet and arching bones, and I watched Nielsen as he whistled over the camp chores. Then I heard the sweet song of a meadow lark, and after that the melodious deep note of a swamp blackbird. These birds evidently were traveling north and had tarried at the oasis.

Lying there I realized that I had come to love the silence, the loneliness, the serenity, even the tragedy of this valley of shadows. Death Valley was one place that could never be popular with men. It had been set apart for the hardy diggers for earthen treasure, and for the wanderers of the wastelands—men who go forth to seek and to find and to face their souls. Perhaps most of them found death. But there was a death in life. Desert travelers learned the secret that men lived too much in the world—that in silence and loneliness and desolation there was something infinite, something hidden from the crowd.